A special thanks to Ameliana

Larry E. O'Neal's books
Available at:
amazon.com/author/larryoneal
(use lowercase letters)

Copyright 2022 by Larry E. O'Neal

Dedication

I dedicate this to the God of Heaven and Earth, through whom all things are possible. I write this for our Heavenly Father, my family, and you.

Philippians 4:8 Finally brethren, whatsoever things are true, whatsoever things are honest, whatsoever things are just, whatsoever things are pure, whatsoever things are lovely, whatsoever things are of good report; if there be any virtue, and if there be any praise, think on these things.

INTRODUCTION

Contained within these pages are events taken from my life. These events are placed here as an example of how God has blessed and kept me. If God has watched over me and kept me, He will certainly do the same for you. That is if you are one of His children. So, Mirror Jesus in all that you think, do, and say, so victory and blessings will be yours. Praise God continually!

I share these events so that you will know what God has brought me through during my life. That way, God will receive the glory for helping me. If He brought me through these things, He would bring you through too.

Throughout my life, there have been challenges. But with God's help, I know that all will be ok. With God, all things are possible. All things are not lost until you lose faith in God. He is the only friend that will stick with you closer than a brother.

Proverbs 18:24 A man that hath friends must shew himself friendly: and there is a friend that sticks closer than a brother.

In this book, you will find events from my life that reflect God's presence. He has been a constant companion, even when I strayed from Him. It is my prayer that I continually seek Him and never stray away from Him. May I forever heed His voice, be obedient to His will, and **Mirror Him**.

Mathew 5:14 You are the light of the world. A city that is set on a hill cannot be hidden.

John 8:12 Then spake Jesus again unto them, saying, I am the light of the world: He that follows me shall not walk in darkness but shall have the light of life.

INDEX

Behind The Eyelid Videos.............................. 1
Hard Noggin... 19
Wingover.. 28
Opossum... 36
Jurassic Creature.. 44
Have Patience.. 52
Gone Fishing.. 65
Decisions Cost.. 72
River Dogs.. 86
River Slide.. 94
The Visitation... 101
The Timekeeper.. 107
Hearts Wishes... 117
Gentle Persuasion...................................... 122
Artificial Intelligence................................. 133
Max.. 153
The Dream.. 165
Borrowed Time... 175
David and Goliath...................................... 192
Early Hour Dream...................................... 198

Behind the Eyelid Videos

Firsts, I believe a little clarification is in order. There is a vast difference between dreams and visions. Yes, dreams can seem real but not as real as a vision, especially when you are fully awake.

I believe that dreams can come from either an overactive or a bored mind. If a person has been working on a vast problem, then an overactive mind could be to blame. It could come from a mind that is bored with nothing to do while you are sleeping.

Then, there is the third kind of dream. This third kind of dream comes from God. My suggestion is to write your dreams down as soon as you have them. Do not wait until you awake in the morning. I think you will be surprised at how many of your dreams will come true sometime in the future. I myself have had many dreams which actually came true.

A vision from God is totally different. In a vision, there is a direct connection with your senses. In a vision, you may see, hear, smell, and feel your surroundings as you normally would. Don't be alarmed, it's just our Heavenly Father getting up close and personal. Believe me, you will know the difference once you have experienced a vision. If you have, write it down and share it with your family.

Although part of the following, may at first seem strange, I can assure you that it is all true. I have never written or wished to write fiction. Why should I, truth is often stranger than fiction.

Several years ago, something strange began happening to me that I cannot fully explain. I started having late-night, behind-the-eyelid videos. Yes, you heard me right. I could close my eyes at night and see patterns of light, pictures, and actual videos.

At first, these pictures and videos were in black and white. Occasionally they were only patterns of light. Then there were times when they were in vivid color. There was, however, no sound during these pictures and videos.

Each pattern, picture, or video lasted only seconds, before being replaced by another image. I could never look directly at these images. Each time I tried to look directly at one, it would drift down and to the right, out of my sight. I always had to look slightly to the edge of these images to be able to tell what I was seeing.

The pictures eventually came during the daytime as well. I only needed to close my eyes for a moment. One day I informed my wife about the images. She thought it was very strange. I closed my eyes and described a scene to her. I do not believe that I had ever seen this exact scene anywhere before. As I began describing the scene, she became incredibly quiet. When I had finished, she was just sitting there looking at me. I wondered; does she think that I was losing touch with reality? Does she think that I need professional help? Did she think I was nuts but was polite enough not to say so?

When I had finished telling her what I saw on the backside of my eyelids, she asked, "What do you think it means"? I replied, "I do not know but it is very interesting". After that, we did not speak about it again. That is until after the event that I am about to tell you of.

I once heard my father-in-law explain how his wife could fall asleep as soon as her head hit her pillow. I replied, "She must have a clear conscience". My wife said that I could also fall asleep very quickly.

I have prayed often during the day. I make sure that I pray before going to sleep. I ask for forgiveness for the things that I have done that have caused God to be displeased with me. I ask for forgiveness for the things that I did not do that I should have done. I ask for forgiveness and protection for my family and myself. I thank Him for the blessings that I have received from Him. I always thank Him for more than I ask for. I believe this helps me have a clear conscience, which helps me fall asleep quicker.

Before tonight, I had fully intended to tell you about the eyelid videos. I hoped that it would help you fall asleep quicker.

After saying your prayers, just close your eyes when you lay down at night. Then, gaze into the darkness of the backside of your eyelids. I would have also told you to count your blessing instead of sheep. Now my suggestion is, to say your prayers, then try watching the eyelid videos.

I would like to offer the following explanation from the Holy Bible.

GOD SEALS INSTRUCTIONS IN MEN AS THEY LAY UPON THEIR BEDS –

Job 4:13 In thoughts from the visions of the night, when deep sleep falls on men.

Job 33:15 In a dream, in a vision of the night, when deep sleep falls upon men, in slumber upon the bed.

Job 33:16 Then he opens the ears of men, and seals their instruction,

Job 33:17 That he may withdraw man from his purpose and hide pride from man.

Job 33:18 He keeps back his soul from the pit and his life from perishing by the sword.

According to the Bible, God gives men instructions that He seals inside of them. We cannot recall at any given moment what those instructions are. It is only at the time of God's choosing that He reveals pieces of those instructions to that person, and then they understand. Scripture tells us that this is to remove pride from man. If a person knew the plans God has for them, this person might strive towards those plans. That would not allow God to work things out the way He wants to. This person may become filled with pride knowing God's plans for them and what they will accomplish in their lifetime. It is only after we have accomplished God's plan that we can look back and see the reason, things happened as they did.

From the very beginning, I was very intrigued by these nightly pictures and videos. The pictures would start in black and white but soon would be displayed in vivid color. This intrigued me even more. These eyelid pictures and videos were a way for me to fall asleep sooner, or so I thought. They were never the same and kept changing before I fell asleep. Each night I would see these eyelid pictures and videos and I looked forward to them.

Just before this event, I had been sick for three or four days. I would wake up in the middle of the night feeling like I was freezing to death. I would be shaking so violently that I could not walk down the hall without holding onto the walls.

Later this morning, I rose out of bed feeling fine except for an overwhelming feeling of tiredness. I let our two dogs out in the backyard for a few minutes. I brought them back inside and returned to bed. The feeling of exhaustion was overwhelming.

Sometime later, I again got out of bed, freezing once again. I was shaking so violently that I could hardly stand. By this time, my wife was up and sitting in the living room. As she observed me trying to walk, she said, "Get dressed, I am taking you to the hospital".

I went to the Emergency Room, two times within four days. They could not find out what was wrong with me. The tests that they performed came back normal. After the two trips to the hospital, my health returned to normal.

I did not have the nightly pictures or videos during the time of illness. But the pictures and videos were soon to return. As I said my nightly prayers, I thanked God for allowing me to see them again. I told Him that I enjoyed the nightly images and looked forward to them. But tonight, they were to reach a level that I simply cannot wait to tell you about.

Years ago, computer monitors had a display screen that displayed an image in one color. They all had black backgrounds and displayed letters forming words that were green, orange, or white in color.

Tonight, my eyelid videos began in monochrome, orange letters on a black background. The first picture appeared as a single line of words. I could not make out what the words said, only knowing that they were words. Then, another line of words appeared over the first line. The second line appeared rotated at a slight angle. Then another line quickly appeared at a slightly different angle. The pace at which these lines appeared, increased to a maddening rate until a design like a ball was constructed.

Moments after the ball was constructed, it vanished. It flew apart in what seemed like an explosion. There was no sound, just the letters flying apart in all directions. Then a similar design was constructed like the one before, for what I initially thought was for my enjoyment. Then, another shape was constructed a little different, but sort of a ball, nevertheless. The lines of words were appearing at an incredible rate of speed and now totally covered each other. Each time a ball was completed, it vanished and another one began. This continued for a while before the images changed.

Now the lines of words were not constructing a ball any longer. Now they were creating geometric shapes that were very strange indeed. Some of the shapes were tall, slightly wider at the bottom than the top. Some were wide at the top and bottom but narrow in the middle. Then these pictures began appearing as, strange DNA strands. Then there were much broader shapes and symbols. Each picture was being created in what looked like a square box.

After several minutes of these shapes and symbols, the picture zoomed out to a much larger picture. There were hundreds of these small squares making up a much larger picture. The ball and geometric-shaped images were only an up-close look at a much smaller single picture. Each square was creating its own unique design.

There were hundreds of these small squares side by side, above and below each other forming one huge square. From time to time, the video would change, and it would zoom in to a different square. It would remain for a minute or so to allow me to see that they were all made up of words. But I still could not make out any of the words. Each time that I tried to look directly at the words, the square would quickly drift down and towards my right out of view.

As it zoomed out to the large square of squares, I noticed something I had not noticed before. I noticed that the images were changing in each of these hundreds of squares at the same time.

Normally I would have fallen asleep within a few minutes, but I was too intrigued for that by now. I watched this for a long time and had to get up to tell you about this. I sprang from my bed to sling words into this document so I would not forget a single detail. I did not think I was losing my mind. I felt like the Lord had been preparing me for this happening. I felt like He was revealing something to me with my previous eyelid pictures and videos.

I will try to keep you posted on my eyelid pictures and videos. But for now, it is getting late, and I cannot wait to see what happens in a couple of minutes when I lay down again. Good night, God Bless, and pleasant dreams

Well, I went back to bed as I said I would. I closed my eyes and thanked God again for letting me see the things that He had shown me. Moments later, it started all over again. The words in these lines flashed into place as though being written by a laser or streaking meteors. Once their strange shape was created, it would flash apart in all directions as dots of light. The dots flashed past and all around me only to appear in front of me again as swirling, spiraling points of light.

Sometimes they would converge into a single point of light only to repeat their dance of beauty again. I watched this happen repeatedly for a long time. Then the video appeared as words scrolling upwards at a rapid rate of speed in a single box.

No, I had not taken a prescription or any medication before lying down. No, I had not eaten any bad pizza. At the time of this writing, I am seventy-one years of age and do not take any prescriptions at all for my health. I also do not take anything to help me sleep. I give God the praise for not having to take medications. By the time this book gets published, I will have reached my seventy-second birthday. God has blessed me greatly and has given me great health and I praise God for that. I can still perform any task that I want to without any problem. My wife says that I get around like a much younger person, to which I say, "Praise God."

Soon, the video changed again. This time it was in full color. The scene now before me was of a beautiful, Chestnut Red, horse. The horse was shinny to the point that it glistened in the sunlight. The horse was standing, grazing in the greenest, most beautiful meadow that I have ever seen. There were green trees on the backside of the meadow. There was one green, tall, healthy oak tree in the middle of the meadow.

The horse's mane and tail were gently moving in a gentle breeze. Every so often, the horse would move a hoof or shift its weight onto another leg. When it moved, rays of light flashed from its muscles. I have never seen a more majestic creature in all my life.

It was after watching this horse for a good while that I realized, this horse too had been created from words. I had not realized this until the words that made up the horse image began peeling away from its rear, upper part. The words began floating away very slowly in the soft breeze and then increased in speed. The words drifted away faster and faster until the video of the horse was gone.

It was then that I again got out of bed to put these sightings into my computer. It was close to one o'clock in the morning by now. With that accomplished, I returned to bed with great anticipation.

As I lie down and close my eyes, the videos began once again. It was a moment later that the first person appeared right in front of me. The only way to describe this person was, he was a Mighty Man of Valor. He was wearing a metal chest plate that was dark in color. The chest plate was covered with ornate decorative symbols. Each symbol was the color of bright polished brass or bronze. Somehow, I knew that these symbols were in recognition of the many battles that he had won.

This person wore a cape around his neck and over his shoulders. There must have been a gentle breeze blowing, as the cape moved ever so slightly behind him. His hair was dark in color, and it too was blowing slightly behind his head. I tried as hard as I could, but I could not see his face.

This person was huge in stature. He had mounds of muscles upon his shoulders and arms. As I tried to hug him, I found that my arms could not reach halfway around him. My head only came up to the bottom of his chest. His arms were as hard as the limb of an oak tree, yet he was very gentle. I had a sense of peace and safety being there with him.

Moments after I saw these things, I realized that there were other men behind him. Each wore a chest plate of armor, of dark bronze color and cloaks as well. They all held huge swords that reflected light that flashed when moved. Every man had huge muscles and flowing hair. Once again, I could not make out any of their faces.

Suddenly there was a video of a mighty battle, silhouetted against a lighter sky. Silhouettes were all that I could see as I watched this battle rage before me. Suddenly, I could hear sounds. I could hear the clanking of swords that reflected light as they were swung. I could hear the verbal sounds of these mighty men as they put forth heroic effort delivering mighty blows with their swords. These Mighty Men of Valor were between me and the enemy.

Occasionally I could see flashes of bronze, reflected light from the men's armor that was closest to me. After several minutes, this video was to vanish as well. Somehow, I knew that these Mighty Men of Valor were fighting this battle to protect me, but why? This raging battle was one that I could never hope to win myself.

Up to this very moment, I have not slept a single wink. It is now close to 2:30 in the morning. I have been seeing all these things as though my eyes were fully open the entire time.

Once again, I sprang from my bed to deliver the sights and sounds to this document. Only then could I return to bed. This was something that I did not want to rely on my memory to tell later.

I had opened my eyes many times during all of this. I looked at the light shining upon my curtain from outside of my window. Each time I would glance at the clock on my nightstand to make absolutely sure that I was not dreaming. No, I was not sleeping as the clock kept advancing. A moment later, I would close my eyes quickly so as not to miss a single thing. By now it is slightly after three o'clock in the morning.

I returned to bed once again. Upon returning to bed this time, I discovered sadly that the eyelid videos were gone now. However, replacing them was the most beautiful choir that I have ever heard in my entire life. I thought, "How wonderful, now God is going to sing me to sleep." But the more I listened the more I wanted to listen. The sound of such great peace and harmony was too incredibly wonderful to put into words.

I listened very intently but they were not singing words. They were singing what seemed to be melodies the entire time. It could have been words that were in their song. Just maybe, it was a language that I did not understand. Could it be the language of Heaven that they were singing?

For the next three hours, I listened to this choir and loved every moment of it. On occasion, I could make out men's voices. I could hear women's voices in the choir as well. Such harmony, such joy, and such peace I have never heard or known, and I did not want it to end. I wished several times that there was a way to record what I was listening to. As I now think back upon the sounds of the choir last night, I feel the presents of God all over me.

I listened to this choir as I lay on my bed until a little after five-thirty in the morning. Then, I reluctantly fell asleep. It was just after six-thirty when I woke with a leg cramp and I had to walk it out.

I returned to my computer to try and describe all that I have been listening to. Oh, if there had only been a way to record what I heard. I would have dearly loved to listen to it again. I would have also purely loved to share those sounds with you. I do not have the words to fully describe the feelings, peace, love, and wonder that flood over me. Nevertheless, I wanted to write this down for you, and I never want to forget any of it.

After I had written everything down, I went to let our three fur babies out in our backyard. Our fur babies consist of three small dogs, Tosha, Sophie, and Luke.

What a shock my wife is going to have when I tell her about this. I simply cannot wait to tell her and my siblings of my night's events.

It is now twelve minutes after nine as I finish writing this. I could not wait to tell others about what I had witnessed. Two of my siblings thought that I had seen glimpses of Heaven. Others did not know what to think. All wanted to know what I thought it was. All I can say is, "I was fully awake the entire time. I can only describe it as a night vision". I only had about one hour of sleep and that was after five-thirty in the morning. To my delight, I have not been tired at all today.

Pray continually and give God the praise and glory for everything in your daily life. Only then will you see the glory of God. The Bible tells us that God inhabits our praise and worship. Praise and worship God without pause and you will feel His presence near you always.

Psalms 22:3 But You are holy, O God you that inhabits the praises of Israel.

The scripture above says Israel, but through Jesus Christ when we become saved, we are adopted into the family of God. Therefore, we have access to the blessings of God as well.

Romans 11:16 For if the first fruit (Jesus Christ) ***is Holy, the lump is also Holy; and if the root*** (Jesus Christ) ***is Holy, so are the branches.***

Romans 11:17 And if some of the branches were broken off, and you, being a wild olive tree, were grafted in among them, and with them became a

partaker of the root and fatness of the olive tree,

Romans 11:18 do not boast against the branches. But if you do boast, remember that you do not support the root, but the root supports you.

God loves us all very deeply. What are you doing to show God how much you love Him? I am aware that everyone has their difficulties. But how much worse would they be without God? Could we even survive without His miracle-working power and daily blessings? I doubt that we could. We would not be able to experience happiness as we do. We would not have the hope of a happier tomorrow. There would be no eternal life for us. But through Jesus Christ, we have the blessings of God. It is only through God's love and His loving grace that we are even here.

John 14:6 Jesus said unto him, I am the way, the truth, and the life: no man comes unto the Father but by Me.

Jesus is the doorway, and we must pass through Him to gain access to our Heavenly Father. Only by accepting Jesus Christ as our personal Lord and Savior can we gain access to our Heavenly Father. *Mirror Him*

Hard Noggin

Psalms 75:5 Lift not up your horn** (head) **on high: speak not with a stiff neck.

It was another one of those typical Florida summer days when the heat seemed to keep rising. As cars sat in the searing sun, you could accidentally burn yourself with your own seat belt buckle. Vinyl seat covers stick to the back of your legs, and the Florida sand spurs were looking for shade.

During the summer in Florida, we have frequent thunderstorms. I was in my third year of school, at the time. There was a soft rain as I disembarked from the school bus and ran home.

I entered our front door and greeted my mother. I had begun to put my book bag down when I heard it. It was just a small sound at first. It only lasted for a moment, but I heard it clearly. Then, I heard it again. It was a sound that I had not heard before and I was very curious as to what was making such a sound. I ran over to the window and looked out to investigate.

There in our backyard were the two goats that we had for a couple of years. Beside one of the goats were two of the most beautiful baby goats that I had ever seen. Yes, our female goat named Nannie had given birth to two baby goats during the thunderstorm. My mother allowed me to go outside and visit with the baby goats the following day.

As the days passed, the baby goats grew and grew. They would run and kick up their heels and run in circles. They had so much fun playing. Watching them made a boy of eight years old want to get involved.

Each day after school, I would hurry home to play with my new baby goats. I would talk and play with them. I would pet them and play with them. In just a few days, they began looking forward to me coming home from school. Each time they saw me come out the back door, they would run to greet me.

Each day I would get down on my hands and knees and chase them, which they loved. On occasion, I would place my forehead against one of theirs and push slightly. I had to be gentle as they were just babies. My mother had warned me saying, "I would not do that if I were you". I found out the hard way that she was right, as usual.

Proverbs 2:1 My son, if thou wilt receive my words, and hide my commandments within thee.

Proverbs 2:2 So that you incline your ears unto wisdom and apply your heart to understanding.

Proverbs 2:3 Yea, if you cry after knowledge and lift your voice for understanding.

Proverbs 2:4 If you seek her as silver and search for her as for hidden treasures.

Proverbs 2:5 Then shalt you understand the fear of the LORD and find the knowledge of God.

Proverbs 2:6 For the LORD gives wisdom: out of his mouth comes knowledge and understanding.

I had arrived home from school that day, dropped my book bag, greeted Mom, and headed to the backyard. My two little friends came running to meet me and we began to play.

After a while and still on my hands and knees, I began to push heads with one of the baby goats. After a couple of pushes, I pushed but the baby goat was not there. Still, on hands and knees, I looked up.

To my surprise, I saw the baby goat that I had been playing with, was now standing on its hind legs. It was holding its front legs close to its chest and its head tilted downward. The baby goat was in attack mode. It all happened so fast, that I had no time to react. Its forehead struck my forehead with such force that it knocked me backward and onto my back. We still played after that, but I refrained from head pushing with the baby goats.

There are people that thought my mother had dropped me when I was a baby. But after hearing this story, they just say "Ah," like now they understand why I am as I am.

Dad had an expression he would sometimes say. He would say, "Two heads are better than one, even if one is a goat's head". I am still trying to figure out exactly what he meant by that one. I did ask him one time, "Are you calling me a goat's head"? He just looked at me and smiled.

Dad had another expression that he would tell me and my siblings. He would say, "Go ahead and butt the wall with your own head." I wonder if he was referring to this goat incident. Perhaps dad simply meant, to go ahead and learn the hard way. One thing is for certain, if we do not listen to good advice, we will certainly learn the hard way. Whatever dad meant, it caused us to pause and reevaluate our thoughts.

Our walk with God is similar to my dad and mother's warnings. God warns us of things that we should refrain from doing. He speaks to us in a small quiet voice and through His Holy Word. But He leaves the decision up to us. If we decide to listen to His warning, we avoid harsh consequences. But if we do not heed His warning, we are in for a hard lesson.

There is an old saying that says "A smart man learns from his own mistakes. A wise man learns from the mistakes of others. But a fool never learns". I would like to add to that if I may. I would like to add, "A fool only blames others".

Please listen to God when He speaks to you. How do you know if that small voice is God that is speaking to you? I am glad that you asked that question. It is often a small quiet voice that seems to come from inside of you. It seems like it is a thought. When God speaks to you, it is NEVER contradictory to His word. If you do not read your Bible daily, you will not know what God's word says. By reading God's word, and being born again, you gain insight into His character.

What does being born again mean? It means asking Jesus Christ to forgive you of all your sins. One must also ask Jesus Christ to be their Lord and Savior. Once you are born again, God's Spirit comes to live inside of you. With God's spirit living inside of you and reading God's word, you will recognize who is talking to you.

John 10:27 My sheep hear my voice, and I know them, and they follow me:

Sometimes, God will speak to you through other people. You may be with someone, and they say something that almost goes without notice. If you do take notice of what they said, compare it with what the Bible says about it. If it lines up with God's word, well and good. If it does not line up with God's word, forget it. Example: Someone says, "Perhaps it would be nice to visit old Mrs. Smith". If you go to visit Ms. Smith, you could ask how she is feeling. Then perhaps you could tell her about God's love for her. Perhaps that word about God will change her life.

On the other hand, you shrug it off and do not go to see Ms. Smith. That night, Ms. Smith passes away. Now you feel regret that you did not tell her that God loves her. That could have been what she needed to hear the most.

Perhaps that little voice says, "Don't go with that person." You heed the voice and do not go. The next day you hear that person did something wrong and is now in jail. Thank God that you listened, or you too would be in trouble.

Often God speaks to you through a parent or grandparent. When they say, "I don't think I would be doing that." Perhaps someone says something like, "That could cause you a problem". That could be God speaking through them, to you. Suggestion: if it lines up with God's word, listen!

Luke 18:16 But Jesus called them unto Him, and said, suffer (let) **the little children to come unto me, and forbid them not: for of such is the kingdom of God.**

Luke 18:17 Verily I say unto you, whosoever shall not receive the kingdom of God as a little child shall in no wise enter therein.

Small children have such gentle and trusting hearts. They receive instruction from their parents and believe what the parent says. Such is the kingdom of God, Jesus tells us. We should trust our Heavenly Father to always have our best interest at heart. We must believe His Holy Word and follow it always.

Yes, God does speak through children to parents occasionally. Children have tender hearts and are willing to listen to God. The world has not yet corrupted children's thinking. God will sometimes speak to a small child when a parent is not listening to Him. The point here is to listen and evaluate what we hear. A wise man once said; ***"If you are talking, you are not listening. If you are not listening, you are not learning"***.

You ask, "What is God's word"? Again, I am glad that you asked. The Holy Bible contains God's word. To understand God, one must read His Holy Word. It gives us an insight into what He thinks, what He likes and does not like. This enables us to stay in His good graces.

Suggestion; study other people. See what they have done right and what they have done that did not work out well. Always follow good examples and separate yourself from the bad examples. Your life will be much better if you follow this simple advice.

Proverbs 1:15 My son, walk not in the way with them; refrain your foot from their path:

Proverbs 1:16 For their feet run to evil and make haste to shed blood.

Psalms 23:4 Yea, though I walk through the valley of the shadow of death, I will fear no evil: for thou art with me; they rod and thy staff they comfort me.

Psalms 23:5 Thou prepares a table before me in the presence of my enemies; Thou anoints my head with oil; my cup runs over.

Psalms 23:6 Surely goodness and mercy shall follow me all the days of my life and I will dwell in the house of the LORD forever.

It is to our advantage to live as close to God as we possibly can. Read His Holy Word daily and live our lives in accordance with His word. Then we can expect His helping hand in our hour of need and trouble. Always trust in Him and your faith will be well-founded. Never let go of His loving hand. Be Greatly Blessed is my prayer for you. *Mirror Him*

The Wingover

Isaiah 40:31 But they that wait upon the Lord shall renew their strength; they shall mount up with wings as eagles; they shall run, and not be weary, and they shall walk, and not faint.

The year was 1969 and I had been in the US Navy for a little more than two years. I had served on the flight deck with an anti-submarine squadron. I was aboard two aircraft carriers the USS Essex and the USS Wasp. While aboard the USS Essex, we recovered the Apollo 7 crew. While aboard the USS Wasp, we visited seven countries in Europe.

After having sea duty for two years, I attended a navy school in Milton, Tennessee, and learned how to work on jet engines. Yes, I was a fledgling jet engine mechanic.

Upon completion of my training, I was assigned to a different kind of antisubmarine squadron. This squadron was land-based in the state of Maryland. They did not have the smaller aircraft that the aircraft carriers had. These aircraft were the P3 Orion type which is a much larger airplane.

The P3 Orion aircraft has four jet turboprop engines. That simply means four jet engines that have propellers. I not only worked on these jet engines but was also part of a flight crew.

With all four engines running, this airplane could fly to its patrol location, shuts down two engines, patrol for hours then restarts the two engines to return home. They did this to conserve fuel which enabled them to stay on patrol longer.

The P3 Orion is one of the airplanes that the National Oceanic and Atmospheric Administration (NOAA for short), use to fly into hurricanes. They are such durable airplanes the P3 Orion is still in use today.

On this day, we were to go on a training flight. The copilot was a seasoned veteran of the squadron, but the pilot was new to the squadron. This was to be his first flight as the pilot in a P3 Orion and he was excited.

Once the flight crew was aboard, it was time for the preflight instructions. The new pilot said, "OK men, today we are going flying, let's go." With that, he turned and headed for the cockpit. The older pilot said, "Wait a minute! Tell them what we are going to do."

The new pilot said, "We are going to fly to a base in Virginia, drop a guy off, then go flying." Once again, he quickly turned and headed towards the cockpit. The older pilot said, "Wait a minute! If we ditch in the ocean, which two men are to take the life rafts out"? The younger pilot quickly pointed to two of us and said, "You take one and you take the other." With that, he turned and rushed to the cockpit.

The older pilot said, "What he told you is true but there is more. We will also be doing a wing-over today, but do not worry I'll let you know before we do it.

"What is a wing-over, you ask"? A wing-over is performed if there is a fire inside the aircraft. With a fire, there is smoke. To remove the smoke and breathe clean air, you must get below thirteen thousand feet to vent the airplane. You vent the airplane by opening a window, door, or overhead hatch. A wing-over is also performed if the airplane loses oxygen pressure. Above thirteen thousand feet, there is not enough oxygen to be able to breathe. Traveling at that altitude, people must carry oxygen with them to breathe.

During a wing-over maneuver, the pilot lowers the wing flaps to slow the aircraft's forward speed. He will also lower the landing gear to slow its forward speed even more. He will then roll the airplane onto its side, dropping one wing tip straight down. He will then point the nose of the airplane towards the ground or ocean. All of this is to get below thirteen thousand feet as quickly as possible. Yes, that will place the airplane in a nosedive, straight down.

After the old pilot told us we were going to do a wing-over, everyone headed to their seats and prepared for takeoff. We flew to a base in Virginia and dropped off the sailor who was going home on leave. We took off and headed northeast out over the Atlantic Ocean in a gradual but steady climb.

As the flight drug on, I became hungry. As with every flight occurring around lunchtime, we had box lunches with us. Eagerly, I opened my box lunch to see what was inside. There was a small carton of milk, a small can of juice, a sandwich, a small bag of chips, and one small candy bar.

The crew member on the other side of the aisle was looking through his box lunch as well. I still had my seat belt securely fastened but he on the other hand was getting very relaxed. He had disconnected his seat belt and was leaning back with legs extended out in front of him. His communications cable was about four feet long and still connected to his helmet.

Somewhere about halfway through my lunch, I heard what sounded like a twig snap. Following that was the sound of an electric motor. As I looked out of the window, I could see the flaps on the wing extending downward. A pilot will use the flaps on the wings to slow the airplane and add lift during takeoffs and landings. I thought, "This is not the wing-over as the older pilot has not warned us".

Moments after that I heard another snap and saw the landing gear come down and lock into place. I thought, "This is not the wing-over because the older pilot hasn't said anything".

In the blink of an eye and without any kind of warning, everything happened suddenly. In one continuous movement, the pilot flipped the airplane onto its side. The right-wing tip now pointed downward, and the nose of the airplane was pointed towards the ocean. It felt as though the bottom had suddenly fallen out of the airplane.

Instantly, I closed my box lunch with one hand and clasp my thumb over the opening of my juice can. With my stomach now firmly lodged in my throat, I thought to myself, "What a ride this is". I knew God was with me, so what could go wrong? Nevertheless, I began to squirm in my seat. My seat and the sailor's seat across the aisle were facing the back of the airplane. Falling backward made everything seem much more intense.

The pilot retracted the landing gear inside the wings. The flaps were retracted as well. The airplane was now screaming towards the ocean at a blinding rate of speed. Imagine if you can, being inside of an airplane the size of a passenger airliner, plummeting towards the ocean. With the airplane now screaming towards the water, all you could do was say a prayer, hold on, and hope the wings did not rip off.

2 Timothy 1:7 For God hath not given us the spirit of fear, but of power, and of love, and of a sound mind.

Hebrews 13:5 Let your conversation be without covetousness; and be content with such things as you have: for He hath said, I will never leave you, nor forsake you.

I looked at the sailor across the aisle from me to see that he was having a much dissimilar experience. There were potato chips drifting in slow motion above his seat. There was a column of milk snaking out of his milk carton like a cobra. The man was drifting about three feet from his seat, facing the ceiling and three feet above the floor. The only thing that was keeping him from drifting away was the intercom cord still connected to his helmet.

It seemed like forever before the pilot began pulling the airplane out of its dive. As he pulled back on the yoke, the airplane leveled out quickly. Oh, the sailor across the aisle? He landed hard on his back against the floor of the airplane. His milk splattered everywhere beside his potato chips.

After five minutes, the older pilot came walking down the aisle, sort of chuckling to himself. He said, "Sorry guys, I forgot to warn you."

Psalms 91:8-10 Only with your eyes will you behold and see the reward of the wicked. Because you have made the LORD, which is my refuge, even the most High, your habitation; There shall no evil befall you, neither shall any plague come near your dwelling.

I take great peace and joy in knowing that God is always with me. He is my God, comforter, protector, provider, healer, friend, advisor, and much more. He has promised to always be with me. Without Him, I can do nothing. For what I am able to accomplish, I give God all the Glory and Praise. It is only by His power and help that we can do anything at all. Without Him, we would not be able to even breathe. Our hearts would not beat, and our eyes would not see. Without Him, we would not be.

John 15:5 Jesus said, "I am the vine, you are the branches: He that lives in me, and I in him, the same brings forth much fruit: for without Me, you can do nothing".

Give God praise continually for He is worthy to be praised. Give Him thanks for all things, both great and small. Let Him guide your every step, remember that He is Lord of all. He is a friend that sticks closer than a brother. He is a constant companion, who loves you deeply. Give Him praise continually. The more that you give Him praise and read His Holy Word, the better you will get to know Him. The more that you get to know Him, the more you will love Him.

Proverbs 18:24 A man that hath friends must shew himself friendly: and there is a friend that sticks closer than a brother. Mirror Him

Opossum

1 Corinthians 7:35 And this I speak for your own profit; not that I may cast a snare upon you, but for that which is good, and that you may give attention unto the Lord without distraction.

During my growing-up years, my dad worked for the railroad. He usually worked what the railroad called a section. A section was simply a section of track miles in length. As a Section Foreman, it was dad's responsibility to supervise a crew that repaired the railway or train tracks.

Sometimes dad would bring home part of his lunch. I looked forward to the occasional hot dog sandwich that mom would make for him. Split two hot dogs length-ways, sear them in a skillet, place a little mustard on two slices of bread and you had a great sandwich. Occasionally, I will fix myself one of these sandwiches and remember.

Dad would sometimes bring other things home that he found at work. Dad would bring things home that would not harm you. Sometimes it was a gopher, better known as a Florida Tortoise. Back in the 1950s, a gopher cooked and placed on rice made a fine meal.

Gophers are now protected by law in Florida, so do not mess with a gopher. Sometimes he would bring home a baby swamp rabbit. These we played with for a bit and then released them into the woods.

Occasionally dad brought things home that you did not want to run loose in your living room. This was to give me and my sisters better knowledge of what to mess with and what to stay away from.

While I was in the second grade, dad returned home one day with a large brown Croker sack. A Croker sack is also known as a burlap bag. My two sisters Sharla, Betsy, and I were very curious as to what the sack held. I was seven years old; Sharla was five and Betsy was about three. Dad sat the sack on the ground and began to untie the cord from around the opening of the sack. We could hear hissing, and growl sounds from inside the sack which made us even more curious.

Dad told us to stand away from the bag. Finally, the sack was untied, and dad dropped the opening of the sack on the ground. To our excitement, there was a lump in the bag that was moving. Wide-eyed with anticipation, we watched the lump move towards the opening of the bag. Then, dad did it! He dumped the contents of the bags in the yard. I first thought it was the largest rat that had ever walked upon the face of the earth. It looked like a rat but was the size of a small dog. It had a tail that looked four feet long, to us kids. But no, it was not a rat. It was an Opossum.

I had never in my life heard such hissing and growling from such a small animal. I was amazed to see a large mouth full of teeth. Its mouth looked more like a chainsaw that was still running. It also had one of the worst attitudes that I had ever seen. But then, if you had placed me in a sack all day, I would be angry too.

I had no idea what we were going to do with this snarling set of teeth. I knew that I did not want to play with this thing. I thought it must be time to experiment a little. I ran into the house and brought out my brand-new fishing rod.

As I approached, my dad cautioned me to stay away from its mouth. I had no intention of getting close to a mouth that seemed so vicious. But I did want to touch the opossum with my new fishing rod to see what it would do.

I approached within reach of the opossum and gently touched its nose with the tip of my new fishing rod. To my surprise, it stopped hissing and growling and pulled its head back. So I touched it again on its nose. It drew its head back even farther.

It was the third touch on its nose that I received a surprise. As I touched it the third time, the opossum's mouth sprang wide open. Its head lunged forward and then its mouth closed. All of this happened before I had time to even flinch. As the opossum drew its head back, it spits out six inches of my brand-new fishing rod. It had bitten the end of my brand-new fishing rod off and spit it back at me. That ended the investigation with the opossum. Dad took the opossum off into the woods and released it.

Satan is exactly like the opossum. He offers you the possibility of what looks like fun. It may look fun and harmless until he has you where he wants you. Then in a blinding display of speed, he springs the trap, and you are in trouble. Sometimes the trouble damage is not too difficult to mend. Sometimes, a simple "I am sorry" will fix it. Other times the trouble damage will cost you time, money, aggravation, sleepless nights, or even wasted years. Sometimes the trouble damage will totally destroy your life. Sometimes, it will end your life. The Bible says, "Satan comes only to steal, kill and destroy".

John 10:10 The thief comes not but for to steal, and to kill, and to destroy: I (Jesus) ***have come that you might have life and that you might have it more abundantly.***

Matthew 10:28 Fear not them which kill the body but are not able to kill the soul: but rather fear him which is able to destroy both soul and body in hell.

With every decision we make, we must ask ourselves, is the cost going to be worth it? How much money will it cost me to mend this decision? Are the consequences going to be worth what looked like fun? How will it weigh on my friends and family? Could it cost me my very life?

Satan has a way of setting a trap or snare for us when we least expect it. We think, my friend did it and nothing bad happened to them. Question: was your friend just lucky or was Satan setting that snare for you and not your friend?

If your friend does not have the calling of God upon their life, then the trap was being set for you. Satan wanted you to see that nothing happened to your friend, so now you think that you can do it. Remember, Satan goes after people that God loves and has great plans for. The greater the plan God has for a person, the greater the attack Satan will plan. But no matter what Satan's plan, always remember that God is with you. God is your strength, refuge, and help in times of trouble. At the same time, we must do all that we can to stay out of trouble. We must make the absolute best decisions that we can all the time.

Please remember, Satan knows you better than you know yourself. Satan will make a suit of temptation that is tailor-made just for you. That suit will fit you better than any other. Be warned!

Proverbs 18:7 A fool's mouth is his destruction, and his lips are the snare of his soul.

Proverbs 29:6 In the transgression of an evil man there is a snare: but the righteous do sing and rejoice.

Proverbs 29:25 The fear of man brings a snare: but whoever puts his trust in the LORD shall be safe.

Ecclesiastes 9:12 For man also knows not his time: as the fishes that are taken in an evil net, and the birds that are caught in the snare; so are the sons of men snared in an evil time, when it falls suddenly upon them.

1 Timothy 3:7 Moreover he must have a good report *(reputation)* ***of them which are without*** *(other people)****; lest he falls into reproach and the snare of the devil.***

1Timothy is saying, be careful who you associate with. Your friends will often lead you into things that you will wish you had not done. Just being with someone who does something wrong, could make you just as guilty as they are.

Who your friends are, says volumes about who you are and your character? By now you may have heard the old saying, "Birds of a feather, flock together." This is so true! You associate with people that have similar interests and likes as you. Choose your friends wisely and be a friend that is full of good choices and of good character. There is no glory in sinfulness or wrong choices.

Another old saying is: "If you lay down with dogs, you get up with fleas." This means, if you associate with people who do not make good choices, you will become like they are. Trouble will be sure to follow a person such as this.

If you find that you have made a poor choice, STOP, and evaluate what you could have done better. What could you have done to make a better decision for a better outcome?

If you have a decision to make, consult God first. Ask Him what He suggests. We make thousands of decisions every day and consult God on all of them. The simplest decision could have a good outcome or the most devastating consequences. The decision is yours. You will either reap blessings or you will pay the price of the consequences. Choose wisely, my friend.

Remember, if you give satan an inch, he will become your ruler. *Mirror Him*

Jurassic Creature

Have you ever had something happen that was scary only to laugh about it later? Well, here is a true story that I think you will enjoy. However, many years later, my wife is still not laughing about it.

Years ago, when our son Brentt was about five years old, we would collect aluminum cans for him. Then on Saturday morning, I would take him to cash the cans in for money. He would receive a couple of dollars on a good day for his cans. That made a boy of five years old feel like a big boy. Then on the way home, we would stop at a convenience store so he could buy something with his money. He bought whatever he wanted, and I bought the cold drinks. This was hopefully to teach him the value of money.

On this Saturday, we had made plans to go to a small town about twenty-five miles away. My family and I got into the car and headed out. We decided to stop at my parent's house which was along the way.

While at mom and dad's, mom told Brentt that she had been saving cans for him. Mom did not tell us that she placed them in paper bags and then sat them beside the driveway. The paper bags had gotten wet after being outside for three or four days. So, mom picked the bags up and placed them inside of a plastic bag. Not knowing this, I picked the plastic bag up and placed it inside the car on the back seat.

We had only gone about two miles after leaving mom's house when it all began. My wife was talking and both of us were ignoring the talking girls in the back seat. That is until one of them yelled, "There's a BIG roach back here". Following that was a loud scream and I knew what that meant. We did not know that a roach had crawled inside mom's paper bag while it was sitting in her yard.

As quickly as I could, I stop the car well off the road and onto the grass. The doors flew open and out ran my wife and both of our girls. They ran as fast as they could to a fence on the other side of a ditch. Their eyes were open wide like they had seen a monster. Gazing back at the car, they stood there with their backs against the fence. All this time my wife was yelling for Brentt to join them at the fence. She kept telling him, "Come over here, that thing will eat you".

I got out and opened the back door. In the backseat, I saw the biggest palmetto cockroach that I have ever seen. That roach was the granddaddy of all roaches. It was at least three inches long and a full inch and a half wide. After my initial surprise and several seconds, I tried to terminate this huge, Jurassic Creature.

As I was about to strike, the roach saw the crack between the side of the car and the end of the back seat. It dove for the crack and made it to safety. That ended the trip instantly.

My wife and both girls finally rejoined Brentt and me in the car, but with different seating arrangements. How my wife was again in the front seat but with her back against the dash. Both of our daughters were also in the front seat with their backs also against the dash. Where was Brentt? He was in the back seat with his bag of cans.

We went straight home, and I gathered my tools as the family went inside the house. I unbolted the rear seat and removed it from the car. I took a new, family-size can of Black Flag ant and roach killer and sprayed everything. I sprayed the entire back seat now sitting on the grass. I sprayed inside the car where the seat had been. I pulled the insulation up and hosed that down as well. I sprayed Black Flag until it was running and dripping from everything.

Under the seat, I found fifteen cents, a pencil, a broken Crayola crayon, and a small hair clip. But no, I did not find the roach. I reinstalled the backseat into the car. I left the doors open a little in hopes that the fumes from the Black Flag would encourage the creature to leave. Come dark, I closed and locked the car doors.

The following morning was Sunday and as usual, we went to church. Everyone had forgotten about the T-Rex size roach. For the hour-plus that we were in church, the car sat in the hot Florida summer sun. It was getting hotter and hotter by the minute inside the car.

After church, our youngest daughter Stacy decided to go with my mom and dad to the burger stand. As soon as we got in our car, I turned the air-conditioner on high. My wife and I along with our daughter Stephanie and son Brentt headed home. We only lived about one mile from the church.

We were turning the last corner at the end of our block when it came from the back seat. It stood everyone's hair on end that was in the car. It was a scream of terror. It was only one word that everyone recognized. That word was **ROACH**!!!!!

I had just finished the turn at the corner and was barely moving. I applied the brakes as my wife turned around to see where the roach was. As she turned, she found herself face to face and nose to nose with the Jurassic Roach.

The temperature in the car had climbed to a stifling level while we were in church. All the roach wanted was a little of that cool air coming from the air-conditioner. It had climbed from its hiding spot and was now resting comfortably on the headrest of my wife's seat. As my wife turned in her seat, it positioned her nose about three inches from the roach's nose. Now, there was another **Scream of terror**.

I instructed my wife to open her door who was now sitting with her back against my right side. My wife by now was frozen with fear. Stephanie was finally able to reach around the seat and get my wife's door open twelve inches or so. I backhanded the roach which launched it towards the partially open door.

To this day I am still convinced that the roach was going fast enough and at the correct angle to make it out the door. However, my wife insisted that it landed in the seat with her. Stephanie and Brentt by this time were running from the car.

Screaming **ROACH** at the top of her lungs, my wife placed both of her feet against the metal door post between the windshield and her door. In this position, she began pushing violently. I was now pinned and being crushed between my door and my wife. I could not move and had no place to go. It felt like my ribs were going to crack at any moment.

After several moments, I was able to put the car's transmission in park, by using my fingertips. With the fingertips of my left hand, I made a big mistake. I lifted my door handle. It was then that I felt like a wet watermelon seed pinched between the thumb and finger. As the door flew open, I felt like I had been squirted out of the car. I landed on my left side in the middle of our street. My wife also fell out. She was now lying on her back, on top of me with her feet in the air and still screaming **ROACH**.

As I fell from the car, my sunglasses had fallen off and landed on the road beside me. In a flash, my wife rolled to one side and off of me. She got to her feet, screamed **ROACH**, and jumped up and down three times. Each time that she came down, she landed right on my sunglasses.

After her jumping on my glasses ended, she headed home on foot a half-block away. She would take four or five steps, jump into the air, scream **ROACH**, then repeat the process.

By this time, people started coming to the door of their houses wondering what was going on. Our two children were following their mother up the street to our house.

I slowly got to my feet and back into the car. I drove the half-a-block home and pulled into the driveway. As I exited our car, I thought I heard something, but I wasn't sure what. I opened our front door and stepped inside. To my right on the floor was one of my wife's shoes. To my left was her other shoe. Slung across the couch was her blouse. Lying over my footstool was her skirt. I looked at our children and they gave me a look that told me, "Don't ask us"!

It was about then that I heard a scream from the other end of the house. Suddenly my wife ran from the hall, through our living room, and into the family room. At this point, she was wearing only her underclothes. When she could run no farther, she jumped into the air, screamed **ROACH**, and ran in the opposite direction. Once she reached the other end of the house, she repeated the processes. It must have taken her five minutes to calm down.

Sometimes, it is not that a creature will harm you. Often, a small creature will cause you to hurt yourself. Sometimes, what we fear most, is fear itself.

Mark 5:36 As soon as Jesus heard the word that was spoken, He said unto the ruler of the synagogue, Be not afraid, only believe.

Psalms 91:7 A thousand may fall at your left side, and ten thousand at your right hand; but harm shall not come close to you.

From that day to this, no one is for sure where the Jurassic Roach went. The only thing that we are sure of is, that was one HUGE roach. We have never seen that roach since.

Use the wisdom that God has given you and be afraid of nothing. God is always there with you looking out for your best interest and safety. Be content and give God thanks for what you have. Do not be greedy or envious of anything. God is a rewarder to those who seek him and keep His word. *Mirror Him*

Have Patience

Proverbs 16:9 A man's heart plans his way, But the LORD directs his steps.

People often make plans concerning their daily lives without giving God a single thought. They take it for granted that they will be here to complete those plans. But God knows what plans He has for each of us.

Yes, God has a master plan. What is God's master plan? I am so glad that you asked. God loves you more than you could ever imagine. His plan is for all who will to come to the saving knowledge of Jesus Christ and be saved. This is the first step towards a wonderful life after this one. However, it is your choice. You have only one of two choices. Accept Jesus Christ as the sacrifice for your sin and be saved or not. Either way, it is your choice. You see, we are all born into and of sin and must be saved. Jesus Christ is that savior! Choosing not to accept Jesus Christ's saving gift, opens the door to the consequences.

John 3:1 There was a man of the Pharisees, named Nicodemus, a ruler of the Jews:

John 3:2 The same came to Jesus by night, and said unto him, Rabbi, we know that you are a teacher come from God: for no man can do these miracles that you do, except God be with him.

John 3:3 Jesus answered and said unto him, Surely, surely, I say unto you, Except a man be born again, he cannot see the kingdom of God.

John 3:4 Nicodemus said unto him, how can a man be born when he is old? Can he enter the second time into his mother's womb, and be born?

John 3:5 Jesus answered, Surely, surely, I say unto you, Except a man be born of water and of the Spirit, he cannot enter into the kingdom of God.

John 3:6 That which is born of the flesh is flesh, and that which is born of the Spirit is spirit.

To be born again, a person must acknowledge that Jesus is the only **begotten** son of God. We must ask for forgiveness of our sins and ask Jesus Christ to be our savior. After this, we must live our lives according to God's Holy Word as our example. Jesus was the only pure and final sacrifice for our sins. Jesus shed His life's blood upon the cross, to save all who would come to Him in prayer, confess that He is the Son of God, ask for forgiveness of our sins, and accept His sacrifice upon the cross.

He has plans for you to accomplish His plan. He will place people in your path that He wants you to speak to. Speak to about what, you ask? About, how God has blessed you. About God's grace and how much He loves you and them. We should speak of God's healing power and about how special they are to God. Do not forget to tell them that He has a plan for their lives as well.

2 Timothy 1:9 Who has saved us, and called us with a holy calling, not according to our works, but according to His own purpose and grace, which was given to us in Christ Jesus before the world began,

Yes, before the world began God knew you. Not only did God know you, but He had a plan for you. He knows the number of hairs you have on your head and the number of days you will be here on earth. Our life here is not ours but loaned to us by God for His purpose. At the same time, He loves us as no other could.

So, God has a plan for you and me? God has chosen and equipped each person to perform specific things for Him and His kingdom. Some people are chosen by God to pastor a church. Some people are chosen by God to teach in a Sunday school class. Some people are chosen to be prayer warriors, to pray for people, and pray that God's will is done. All are chosen to tell others what God has done for us in our lives. If you do not tell others what God has done for you, how will they know how great our God is?

1 Timothy 2:1 I exhort, therefore, that first of all, supplications, prayers, intercessions, and giving of thanks, be made for all men.

1 Timothy 2:2 or kings, and for all that are in authority; that we may lead a quiet and peaceable life in all godliness and honesty.

1 Timothy 2:3 For this is good and acceptable in the sight of God our Savior.

1 Timothy 2:4 Who will have all men to be saved, and to come unto the knowledge of the truth.

1 Timothy 2:5 For there is one God, and one mediator between God and men, that is Christ Jesus,

1 Timothy 2:6 Who gave himself as a ransom for all, to be testified (told of) *in due time.*

1 Timothy 2: Whereunto I am ordained a preacher, and an apostle, a teacher of the Gentiles in faith and truth.

Romans 8:28 And we know that all things work together for good to them that love God, to them who are the called according to His purpose.

We were created by God for His purpose and not our own. If we remain in His purpose, we remain in His blessings. When something comes our way that we consider not a blessing, we have God as a constant companion to help us. It is by His strength and not our own that we get through this life.

It is when we step out of the will of God that our problems begin. The longer a person stays out of the will of God, the worse their problems become. Their problems become so hard that it is difficult for them to see their way back to where they belong. This is where you and I come in. You and I speak to and remind them that God loves them, and He wants the absolute best for them. Remind them that no matter what happens, God has promised us that He will never leave us. We may leave Him, but He will never leave us unless we send Him away. How do we send Him away? We send Him away by continually rejecting Him and His teachings.

Genesis 6:3 And the LORD said, "My spirit shall not always strive with man, for that he also is flesh: yet his days shall be a hundred and twenty years."

Romans 1:25 Who changed the truth of God into a lie and worshiped and served the creature more than the Creator, who is blessed forever. Amen.

Romans 1:26 For this cause God gave them up unto vile affections: for even their women did change the natural use into that which is against nature:

Romans 1:27 And likewise also the men, leaving the natural use of the woman, burned in their lust one toward another; men with men working that which is unseemly, and receiving in themselves that recompense of their error which was meet.

Romans 1:28 And even as they did not like to retain God in their knowledge, God gave them over to a reprobate mind, to do those things which are not convenient;

Romans 1:29 Being filled with all unrighteousness, fornication, wickedness, covetousness, maliciousness; full of envy, murder, debate, deceit, malignity; whisperers,

Romans 1:30 Backbiters, haters of God, despiteful, proud, boasters, inventors of evil things, disobedient to parents,

Romans 1:31 Without understanding, covenant-breakers, without natural affection, implacable, unmerciful:

Romans 1:32 Who knowing the judgment of God, that they which commit such things are worthy of death, not only do the same but have pleasure in them that do them

If one does these things and continues to reject God, He will turn them over to a reprobate mind. What does that mean? It means; that God will cause them to believe Satan's lies and be lost to sin forever. There is a breaking point. There is a point where God will reject a person if they continue to reject Him.

Where do we belong? We are all God's creations, and we belong in His loving embrace. We belong covered in His tender mercies, forgiveness, and purpose. There is peace, joy, hope, and assurance of a wonderful eternity with Him. But only if we are living for God and are where we are supposed to be. Being close to God and in His will, brings us the personal help of God Himself. But if we are not living in His will, we bring misfortune upon ourselves and even worse things. It is entirely our choice! We cannot blame our circumstances upon God. No matter what our situation may be, it is still our choice as to how we arrived there.

In 2017, I had driven to my mother-in-law and father-in-law's house to do a little work. After I was there for a few minutes, I realized that I had forgotten a tool at home. I drove home, collected the tool, and headed back. Going to their house the first time, I had taken the truck route around town. This time I had decided to take a path through our small town.

As I approached a traffic light, it turned red, and I stopped. There was a new car stopped in front of me, which still had a temporary license plate. Both of us had intended on making a left-hand turn and were in the turning lane.

I watch as the cars stopped for the light on the opposite side of the intersection. The light soon turned green, and the cars began coming across the intersection.

As I watched, a large gap between the cars appeared. The car in front of me just sat there. I impatiently thought, "Person on their cell phone". I gave a friendly little toot of my horn, but the car did not budge. I looked at the oncoming traffic again. I watch as a large, older car moved into the turning lane creating a much larger gap in traffic than before. I anxiously looked at the end of that gap in traffic.

Everything seemed to happen in a blink of an eye. Yes, the older car coming towards us had moved into the turning lane, but the car did not turn. That car slammed into the car in front of me head-on at thirty miles an hour. That does not seem very fast but with all that weight, it was enough to ram the car backward into my truck.

The impact popped both of my airbags before I could blink an eye. It took a moment, for me to realize what had happened. I ran up to check on the woman in the car in front of me. She was injured and needed medical attention, so I called 911. I then checked on the guy who caused the wreck. He was fine but said he had no idea why he did not turn. Within minutes, the woman was transported to a local hospital. Me? I did not even have the powder from the airbags on me. I was without a scratch or bruise.

It was then that I realized God had protected me. If the woman had completed her turn when I thought she should have, I would have received what she got. She received the full brunt of the head-on collision in her new car. As a result, she was transported to the hospital, and I was not.

Because of this wreck, all three vehicles were totaled. I was blessed by God within a couple of weeks with another truck better than the one I had lost. God is so good. He protects us, provides for us and He loves us deeply.

We have no idea what is just around the next corner waiting for us. We have no idea what is on the other side of the intersection. But I know who my protector, provider, and healer is, it's God, my Heavenly Father.

Matthew 8:13 Then Jesus said to the centurion, "Go your way; and as you have believed, so let it be done for you." And his servant was healed that same hour.

I have a protector who knows all from the beginning to the end. He knows what is going to happen, when, and where. Sometimes God changes our route, so we avoid an accident altogether. Other times, we do not know why He allows it to happen, but He is still watching over us. We should look for things to thank God for. Yes, I was in an auto accident. Yes, three vehicles were totaled but I was not injured. We should share with others what

God has done for us. We will be rewarded for these things if we live our lives for Him.

I give God the praise and glory for taking care of, protecting, providing for, and healing me. He has taken care of me all my life and He will do the same for you.

Jeremiah 29:11 "For I know the plans I have for you," says the LORD. "They are plans for good and not for disaster, to give you a future and a hope.

Psalms 9:1 I will praise you, LORD, with all my heart; I will tell of all the marvelous things you have done.

Psalms 104:33 I will sing to the LORD as long as I live. I will praise my God to my last breath!

I heard a story once about a person who was riding in a car. Suddenly a car came out of a side road right in front of them and a crash was inevitable. The passenger shouted out the name of Jesus as the cars collided. That person told me that it was as though they had fallen face-first onto a feather bed. They attributed it to their guarding angel wrapping its wings around them to cushion the impact. This person was not injured in the car crash, and it totally destroyed both vehicles. -

Do not allow anyone to explain away your miracle!! Too often people who are not Christians will do that. Sometimes it is intentional and sometimes it is from not understanding. There are people who have become brainwashed to believe only that which can be explained by science. But God does not operate according to the rules of science. My God is still in the miracle-working business.

Man has devised a set of rules to explain why things happen as they do. Those rules change day by day as man's knowledge expands. But God's rules never change. When something happens that they cannot explain, scientists, create a new rule to alter an old rule. Before long they have ruled God completely out of the picture. They have created so many rules that they cannot remember all of them themselves. It is no wonder that people are so confused. When something good happens that they cannot explain, they should call it a miracle. Then and only then will God receive the praise and glory for what He has done.

God created the rules before men were ever created. God will never work outside of His rules. It is to our advantage to learn what God's rules are and remain within them. How do we do that, you ask? Well, I am glad that you asked. Answer: We must read the Holy Word of God, the Bible. That Bible must have the word **begotten** in *John 3:16* No other Bible will do! If the word **begotten** is not in **John 3:16**, put that book back on the shelf.

Malachi 3:6 For I am the Lord, I change not; therefore, you sons of Jacob are not consumed.

Hebrews 13:8 Jesus Christ the same yesterday, and today, and forever.

My God is a miracle-working god. He is the same today as He was in the beginning. He will remain the same forever. His rules will remain the same and will never change due to circumstances or someone's preferences.

Hebrews 13:7 Remember those who rule over you, who have spoken the word of God to you, whose faith follow, considering the outcome of their conduct.

Hebrews 13:8 Jesus Christ is the same yesterday, today, and forever.

Mirror Him

Gone Fishing

Matthew 4:19 And He said unto them, Follow Me, and I will make you fishers of men.

It was to be another one of those summer days filled with God's love and blessings. Two of my grandsons, Logan and Tyler had arrived at my house before dawn. At the time, Logan was seventeen and Tyler twelve years old. The two of them had decided they wanted to go fishing and had extended an invitation to me. I think that they invited me because I was the only one that had a boat.

After Logan and Tyler arrived at my house, we placed the rod and reels in the back of my truck. We placed the fishing rods beside our tackle boxes which contained an assortment of lures. We were now ready to create good memories.

We drove to where I kept my boat and loaded it on a utility trailer. Today we needed the utility trailer as the boat trailer needed minor repairs. I tied the bow of the boat to the front of the trailer with a good strong rope. With the bow of the boat tied down, we headed down the road.

Within minutes a friendly conversation was underway with great anticipation. The sun had not broken over the eastern horizon yet. We continued along the winding narrow paved road towards a small settlement of houses. This settlement was too small to have a name. Here there are two convince stores, one fire station, and a double handful of houses.

It was about then that the headlights of the pickup truck behind me suddenly but briefly disappeared. In a split second, I knew what had happened but was hoping that it had not. Something told me that the aluminum boat had flipped into the air backward from the trailer.

As quickly and safely as possible, I pulled off the road and looked behind us. Was the boat stuck in the windshield of the truck that had been following me? Had anyone veered off the road to avoid the flying boat? Was anybody injured? Thoughts raced through my mind as I opened my driver's door.

In the dim light of breaking day, I could see the boat lying off to the side of the road. Apparently, the single tie-down rope had somehow come untied. It seemed to be lying softly in the grass, patiently waiting for someone to retrieve it. I thought, "Thank God no one was injured, and it had not caused an accident".

As Logan and Tyler helped me lift it back onto the utility trailer, I looked for boat damage. The boat appeared to have no damage, only a scuff mark or two. So, we double-tied the boat back on the trailer and continued to the lake.

We arrived at the lake and got ready to place the boat into the water. As we gently slipped it into the water, Logan said, "Granddad, we have a leak". When the boat went flying from the trailer, the impact had been worse than I first thought. One of the rivets holding a stiffening rib in the bottom of the boat was leaking badly. I thought, "This fishing trip is over before it began".

It was then that I noticed the expression of great disappointment on both of my grandson's faces. I thought, "Lord, what am I going to do now? I do not want to disappoint these boys".

We tried to place a rock under the rivet and flatten its opposite side. The rivet fell out leaving a hole almost the size of a pencil. I thought, "Lord, what am I going to do now"?

It was then that God reminded me of a small plastic box that I had in my truck. The small box was on the back floorboard. I had been performing work at my son Brentt's house and placed leftover supplies in my truck. Inside that small plastic box were small nuts and bolts. I checked the box and found a bolt the same diameter as the rivet. I also found a nut to go with the bolt. I placed the bolt through the hole, placed the nut on the other side, and tightened them together.

God knew in advance that I was going to need a nut and bolt for this fix. He caused me to place the leftover supplies in my truck. So, you ask, "why didn't God prevent the boat from coming off of the trailer, to begin with?" Well, if God had prevented it, I would not have a blessing from God to tell you about now. It was also a good life lesson for the boys.

Soon, we had the boat back in the water and the quick fix seemed to do the trick. There was only a very minor leak around the bolt. Every now and then, someone had to bail a cup or two of water out of the boat, but we were having fun.

Quickly, both guys had all but forgotten about the missing rivet. In fact, now their attention was fixed on a baby alligator that was cruising nearby. From the middle of the boat, Tyler was saying, "Come here little alligator". The alligator, about a foot and a half long, was lying in the water twenty feet from the front of the boat. I kept telling Tyler, "Leave the alligator alone"! Being the fizzle-dinker that he is, Tyler kept saying, "Come here little alligator" and the baby alligator kept inching closer. I told Tyler, "You need to be careful. A baby alligator that small has a large mother somewhere close by".

Logan was sitting in the front of the boat and was the closest to the baby alligator. As Tyler kept calling the baby alligator closer, Logan kept saying, "If it gets any closer, I am going to whack it on the head with my fishing rod."

It was then that I remembered touching an Opossum on the nose with my new fishing rod. I also remembered what happened to my new rod. I kept paddling the boat slowly backward away from the alligator, but it kept getting closer. Eventually, Tyler stopped trying to encourage the baby alligator to come closer. The little alligator soon lost interest and swam off.

During our morning fishing trip, I had not foreseen the boat flying off the trailer. I had also not foreseen a rivet coming out of the boat causing a leak. I certainly did not think that one of my grandsons would try to get acquainted with a baby alligator. My grandsons and I always have fun together no matter what we are doing. Yes, it was a blessed day that we will remember.

I read years ago, that two friends had gone fishing. Somewhere along the way, a leak had appeared in their boat. To plug the hole and keep fishing, they melted a plastic fishing worm with a cigarette lighter. Once the melted plastic was applied to the leak, they were able to continue fishing.

I had not remembered this while patching our hole with the bolt and nut. Had I remembered it, I would have melted a plastic fishing worm around the bolt first. That would have made the hole entirely watertight.

I mention this now in hopes that I can pass on this tidbit of wisdom to you. May you have a lifetime of good fishing and happy memories with someone you love.

Romans 8:28 And we know that all things work together for good to them that love God, to them who are the called according to his purpose.

Remember, a good fishing trip is not defined by catching a large number of fish. However, catching fish does increase the fun. It is about being with the ones you love and the great memories you create. I wish you many happy hours doing something enjoyable with the ones you love and making wonderful memories. Good memories will be worth an enormous amount in the future to you and others.

Always remember what Jesus Christ did for you and me. Give Him praise and thanks for doing what no one else could have. He is our only hope of being saved from the wrath that is to come. It is only through His loving mercies that we will be saved. Give Him praise continually.

The Bible says, "Sing to Him a new song." That means to make up a new song about the blessings He has given you. Sing from your heart always. It doesn't matter if it doesn't rhyme, it's the thought that counts and that it came from your heart. It does not even matter if you sing out of key. The Bible says, "Make a joyful noise to the Lord." In key or out of tune, He will love it if the song of praise and thanks comes from your heart. What, you don't like to sing in front of people? Then sing in the shower when you are alone. *Mirror Him*

Decisions Cost

Jonah 1:17 Now the LORD had prepared a great fish to swallow up Jonah. And Jonah was in the belly of the fish three days and three nights.

Jonah was a man of God but had a mind of his own. God instructed Jonah to go to a town called Nineveh and preach. Jonah decided that he did not want to go to Nineveh and plotted a different course. Remember that we all have a choice, but it is always better to listen to and obey God.

Jonah bought passage aboard a ship and headed in a different direction. It was not long before a great storm arose, and the ship was about to sink. The men aboard the ship decided that Jonah was the cause of the storm and their peril. To save themselves, they threw Jonah overboard. Instantly, the sea became calm.

God sent a great fish to swallow Jonah and he remained in the fish's stomach for three days. After three days, God caused the fish to get sick and it vomited Jonah upon the shore. After that, Jonah changed his mind, and went to Nineveh and preached.

Proverbs 21:2 Every way of a man is right in his own eyes: but the LORD ponders the hearts.

Why do people resist good advice until things go from bad, to worse? Wouldn't it be much better to do what God asks us to do, to begin with? Yes, God gave each of us free will. But we get to decide things for ourselves. Wouldn't it be much better to ask God what He prefers us to do before we make a decision? Asking Him what he prefers, would eliminate many of our difficulties. Quite often the Bible has the answer to our questions. If we read the Bible, we would know what God's instructions and wishes are.

Today, God does not cause the sea to part or a huge fish to swallow people and they survive. He allows us to decide for ourselves if we want to obey Him. Yes, there is something that He wants each of us to do for Him. But we get to decide if we want to do it. If we decide that we do not want to obey Him, we suffer the consequences of our decision.

Sometimes we get so involved in what is going on, that we forget to listen to God. That is when God reminds us that He is still in control of all things. That is when consequences come about, and we must once again call upon Him. I choose to obey Him first, how about you?

God will equip you to perform His tasks. He will give you a talent or ability to do what He requires you to do. If you decide not to obey God, He will give your talent to someone else. If they perform His task, they will receive His blessings. It is then that you miss God's blessings. Wouldn't it be better for you to receive blessings instead of consequences?

I was once extremely shy and all through school disliked English classes. I took typing classes while in high school just to be in a classroom full of girls. I had no idea that for twenty-five years, I would earn my living typing on a computer keyboard. English classes also enabled me to write this for you. Sometimes we think we are doing something for one reason when all the while, God is preparing us for His work.

Today I have no difficulty speaking in front of people. At the age of seventy, I became a Christian Author so I could share God's love with you. I give God the praise and glory for being able to share this and publish it. While in school, I would have never dreamed that I would be sharing this with you now for God.

Every decision that you will ever make will cost you something. Good decisions will help you escape difficulties and worries. Sometimes people travel through life as though they have no plan. Each day they rise out of bed without any direction. They go about their day bouncing from one thing to another.

They react to things and situations that pop up in their life. They make snap decisions without any thought. They think they have a plan, but they really do not. They think, today I will go to work. Tomorrow I will wash my car. This weekend, I will go to the beach. But what if tomorrow never comes? What will become of all those plans? Where will you be throughout your next life? Yes, you will have an eternal life but where will it be? Your eternal life will be either in heaven or hell, which will you choose?

On occasion, people make decisions without even realizing that they have made one. They think that they will think about it and decide later. At that moment, they have made the decision not to decide for now.

While postponing a decision may be a good thing in some situations, it is never good to make a habit of it. If you keep postponing decisions, they will pile up. Once they begin to pile up, they have a way of becoming overwhelming. Overwhelming simply means that it is difficult to think, as each item clouds the next.

When multiple things become overwhelming, we often make poor decisions as we cannot think clearly. For that reason, it is better to make an intelligent decision now with God's help than to postpone. Postpone a decision only long enough to pray about it and receive an answer from God. My mother always said, "Any decision worth considering is worth praying about".

To be able to make an intelligent decision, we must have the right influences in our lives. We must be mindful of the character of the people that we associate with. We must be mindful of the things that we look at such as books, movies, and TV programs. We must be mindful of the things that we listen to. These things influence our own character, the way we act, talk, and our decision-making.

There are other things that will keep you from making intelligent decisions. Any type of drink containing alcohol in it will cloud your mind. Drugs will also cloud a person's mind. This clouding of the mind will cause a person to make incorrect decisions as well. When these things are present, a person may believe that they have made the best choice. It may only be after the damage is done; do they realize that they have made an incorrect choice.

Sometimes a person does not realize that damage has been done to their lives until years have passed. That is the way Satan wants it. If a person cannot think correctly, they will stay victims of what Satan has for them.

John 10:10 Jesus said, "The thief comes to steal, and to kill, and to destroy: I have come that they might have life and that they might have it more abundantly."

Remember, Satan comes only to kill, steal, and destroy. Who does Satan want to kill? Answer: You and me! What does Satan want to steal? Satan wants to take everything that he can take from you and that includes your health, joy, happiness, and eternal life. What does Satan want to destroy? He wants to destroy God's creation, and that also means you and me. Why does Satan hate you and me so much? Because God created us in His own image. Satan also hates us intensely because God loves us so deeply.

Genesis 1:27 So God created man in his own image, in the image of God created He him; male and female created He them.

That scripture does not say, "Created in the likeness of slime in a primordial soup. It does not say, in the form of a primate or monkey changed by evolution. The Bible says we were created in God's own image. You and I were wonderfully made by a loving God who is full of knowledge and wisdom. He wanted us to look just like Him and I find that to be a wonderful thing.

We must work very diligently and be sure that we do not cause damage that cannot be undone. Only forgiveness from God will cover all sin and allow us to move into God's loving presence. It is only when we forgive others that God can forgive us.

Matthew 18:21 Then Peter came to him and asked, "Lord, how often should I forgive someone who sins against me? Seven times?"

Matthew 18:22 "No, not seven times," Jesus replied, "but seventy times seven!

Mathew 18:23-35 tells the story of a king who wanted to bring his accounts up to date. He summoned a man to be brought before him who owed him a great deal of money.

The man could not pay his debt, so the king ordered that he be sold along with his wife, his children, and everything he owned to pay the debt. But the man fell down before the king and begged him, "Please, be patient with me, and I will pay it all." Please remember that our decisions not only affect us but also our family.

Then the king was filled with pity for him, and he released him and forgave his debt. But when the man left the king, he went to a fellow servant who owed him a small amount of money. He grabbed him by the throat and demanded instant payment.

His fellow servant fell down before him and begged for a little more time. "Be patient with me, and I will pay it," he pleaded. But the man would not wait. He had the man arrested and put in prison until the debt could be paid in full.

When some of the other servants saw this, they were terribly upset. They went to the king and told him everything that had happened. The king called in the man he had forgiven and said, "You evil servant! I forgave you of a tremendous debt because you pleaded with me. Shouldn't you have mercy on your fellow servant, just as I had mercy on you"? Then the angry king sent the man to prison until he had paid his entire debt.

Our Heavenly Father will not forgive us if we refuse to forgive others." We must forgive others to be forgiven by our Heavenly Father

Realizing that we have made an incorrect choice, we have taken the first step to correct it. Often, it is only after our mind becomes unclouded do we truly realize how far we have drifted from God and His path.

1 John 2:1-3 My little children, these things write I unto you, that you sin not. And if any man sin, we have an advocate with the Father, Jesus Christ the righteous: And He is the propitiation (advocate between us and God) ***for our sins: and not for ours only, but also for the sins of the whole world. And hereby we do know that we know Him if we keep His commandments.***

"Forgiveness"? you ask. "How can I forgive them for what they have done"? Jesus Christ died on the cross for all of our sins. He paid our sin debt to save us. He did it because He loves us so much. If we choose Him to be our Lord and Savior, we don't have to pay the sin debt ourselves.

Mathew 26:52 *Then said Jesus unto him, put up again your sword into its place:*

for all they that take the sword shall perish with the sword.

Mathew 26:53 You think that I cannot now pray to my Father, and he shall presently give me more than twelve legions of angels?

According to Google, one legion is equal to 6,000. So, if you multiply 6,000 times twelve, we discover that twelve legions of angels equal a minimum of 72,000 angels. Just one angel has unbelievable strength and ability. Can you imagine what 72,000 angles could do?

Jesus could have summoned at least 72,000 angels to save Him from being crucified upon the cross. If that had happened, all the armies on earth could not have stopped them. So why didn't He save Himself? Because if He had, He would not have provided a way for us to be saved. He was sacrificed, crucified for our sins, so we could be forgiven. Jesus freely gave Himself for you and me. He did not deserve the abuse and death.

Then, on the third day, He arose from the grave showing us that there is life after this one. There is an eternal life with Him or with Satan, it is your choice. There is no other option.

Mathew 6:12 And forgive us our debts, as we forgive our debtors.

Mathew 6:14 For if ye forgive men their trespasses, your heavenly Father will also forgive you:

Mathew 6:15 But if you forgive not men their trespasses, neither will your Father forgive your trespasses.

We must forgive others because Jesus Christ forgives us. We must forgive so that we can receive forgiveness. From time-to-time forgiveness is something that every one of us needs. We need forgiveness from each other and from our God.

Every decision that you will ever make will cost you something. If we make a decision that brings us happiness and joy, then we have made a good decision. If we make a poor choice, we may find that it will cost us money, separation from family, unhappiness, stress, a sense of wasted time, and unhappy eternal life. Which would you rather have, happiness or unhappiness? A poor decision could even cost you your very life.

What gives you happiness? Is it money, a new car, a nice house, respect, spending time with family and friends? What gives me happiness is worshiping God, peace, joy, a loving family, good friends, and a good night's sleep. I also have assurance from God that if I love Him and obey His word, I will have a blessed and happy eternal life with Him. These assurances from Him, give me happiness, what about you?

Mathew 7:13-14 Enter you in at the strait gate: for wide is the gate, and broad is the way, that leads to destruction, and many there be which go in there at Because strait is the gate, and narrow is the way, which leads unto life, and few there be that find it.

Life is like a road trip. We are where we are because of a choice or choices that we have made in the past. If we make a wrong turn while on our road of life, we will become lost. To arrive at our desired destination, we must take the correct path or make the correct decisions.

Once we have made a wrong turn, we must decide, with God's help, the correct course of action to take to get back on the correct road. It may be a difficult struggle to return to the correct path but with God's help, we can do it. Once we know the correct action to take, we must not stray from God's path again.

John 5:14 Afterward Jesus found him in the temple, and said unto him, Behold, you are made whole: sin no more, lest a worse thing come unto you.

You may say, "It was not my fault. I did nothing wrong," and you truly may not have. But you made the decision to go somewhere. While you were there something happened that was not your fault, but you were there. Had you not made the decision to go there, would that something still have happened? If it still happened but you were not there, you would not be involved. Doesn't that sound logical to you? Be careful where you go and with whom.

Be extremely cautious of where you go and with whom you associate. My mother use to tell me, "If you are not looking for trouble, trouble is looking for you". Always remember, evil will always find a way to involve you, but only if you allow it. Stay away from people, places, and things that could cause you problems.

Proverbs 22:1 A good name* is *rather to be chosen than great riches*, and *loving favor rather than silver and gold.

I have heard where someone was with friends and their friend broke the law. This person had no idea that their friend was going to break the law. They had just been hanging out with them, laughing, and having fun. Nevertheless, one person in that group did something wrong. It was as though they had all committed the crime.

Know the character of your friends. Only surround yourself with good people of good character and make good choices. Always ask yourself, what is this decision going to cost me? I once heard someone say, "Satan will take you to places that you did not want to go, keep you there longer than you want to stay, and cost you more than you want to pay".

Once again, be extremely cautious of where you go, who you are with, what you listen to, and what you see. You are the only one who can control these things. You can control much more than you think you can. Ask God to help you make good choices and decisions. Make every decision with God's help.

James 1:5 If any of you lack wisdom, let him ask of God, that gives to all men liberally, and holds back not; and it shall be given him.

On the other hand, if you are not a child of God, that small voice you hear could be Satan. Satan will help you make all the wrong choices. That is a scary thought, isn't it? Become a child of God and know where that small voice inside of you is coming from. Become a child of God and have the help of God.

The question now is, how do you become a child of God? Answer: By asking Jesus Christ to forgive you of your sins, to be your Lord and Savior, and live your life for Him. You should read the Holy Bible and talk to God daily.

Mirror Him

River Dogs

When my son was a youth, he wanted to play baseball. At the age of five years old, we registered him to play T-Ball in the local Little League. Within a couple of weeks, after practice began, I was asked to be an assistant coach. I continued to be an assistant coach or head coach for many years after that.

I enjoyed coaching as it allowed me to share skills and sportsmanship with the youth of our Little League team. Every chance I got, I would also share with them a good word from God.

After our son went through the Little League, I thought my coaching days were over. It was years after that our son had a son of his own. We watched Logan grow as we shared our love with him. By the age of two and a half years old, Logan was using a plastic bat to hit a tossed Nerf ball across our front yard. People would walk by, stop, and watch. Then they would ask how old he was. "That boy is going to be a great baseball player one day" they would say.

When he was five years old, his mother announced that she had registered him for T-Ball in the Little League. We were happy for his chance to play ball as his dad had done years before.

A week later, Logan went to his first T-Ball practice. The following morning his mother called my office. Excitedly she informed me that she had taken him to his first practice which went well. After practice, Logan's coach handed her the team equipment bag and informed her that he was gone. He explained that his grandfather in Puerto Rico was dying, and he did not know when he would be back. Logan's mother explained that she had never coached a T-ball team. I said, "Remain calm, I will help you."

I arrived at Logan's second baseball practice and discovered that his team had an unusual name. Somehow these precious, sweet little faces were given the name, River Dogs. But what is in a name? It still gave me the chance to share skills and God's blessing with them.

Before every practice and every game, we had a quick word of prayer. I would say, "OK, grab a knee," and the children would gather in a circle. While we all knelt on one knee, I would say a short prayer. I usually said something like, "Thank you Lord for a chance to play baseball. Please help us to have a safe game and have fun. Amen." We have chances to let our light shine for God and influence people in a positive way. Never let a chance to praise God slip through your fingers.

For the next several years I would remain either the head coach or an assistant coach for our grandson Logan's baseball team. In fact, his dad and I both coached for years for Logan and his team. It was awesome for his dad Brentt and I to be able to coach together. Our team was the only team in our town to have three generations on the same team.

A couple of years later, Logan's baseball team became division champions. His team was able to play in the regional championship games. During the regional game, I was not one of Logan's coaches. The normal coaches had been replaced, by those who were on the board of directors.

The other team was up to bat and our team was outfield. I was standing several feet from the end of our dugout. Leaning against the outside of the fence, I was watching and instructing an outfielder to move a little to his left. I was not paying attention to the pitcher or batter.

The pitch was thrown, and the batter swung hard. The bat smashed into the ball, and it was a line drive. As the baseball went streaking through the air, it was heading straight towards my head. I had no idea what was going on with the batter as I still had my eyes on the outfielder.

As I stood there oblivious to the fast-approaching baseball, God saw that I was about to experience a problem. God came to my rescue once again.

Heidi is the mother of Riley, one of the young men on our team. Heidi was standing a couple of feet from me, and she was watching the batter. Seeing what was about to happen, Heidi sprang into action. Before I knew what was happening, Heidi quickly grabbed me and snatched me to one side. It was God using her that allowed the baseball to pass harmlessly within inches of my head. As I realized what had just happened, I thanked her for rescuing me and said, "Next time you want to dance, just ask".

God is so wonderful. He knows what is going to happen before it happens. Often, He will place people close by to assist us. We must be observant and recognize those things of God. We must always give God praise for the blessings that he bestows upon us. We should always tell others what God has done for us. That way He receives the praise and glory for helping us. We must never take the praise that

God should have received. If we do, we will cause extreme problems for ourselves.

I heard a story about a man who once became deathly sick. The man had been out of work for weeks. He received prayer and he received a miracle healing. Within days, he was able to return to work. But as the man walked through the gate at work, the guard asked him "What happened to you"? The man replied, "Oh nothing". Instantly, the man fell dead.

Always be quick to give God the glory. What exactly does that mean? It means, tell others what God has done for you. Thank Him each time you remember His helping hands.

Always give God the credit for what He has done. Then people will know that the Bible is true, and it will help build their faith. God is the same yesterday, today, and forever. What He did in the Old and New Testament, He can and is still doing today.

You can plainly see His miracles and helping hand if you are in the right place. Where is the right place, you ask? The right place is the place you belong. The right place is in a good faith church, with good Christians. The right place is also living your life according to His holy word, the Bible.

Are there bad Christians? There are people who call themselves Christians but do not act like it. They continue to hang on to the things of this world and Satan. If you saw the way they act during the week, you would not call them a Christian.

Deuteronomy 4:9 Only take heed to yourself, and keep your soul diligently, lest you forget the good things which your eyes have seen, and lest those things depart from your heart all the days of your life: but teach them to thy sons, and thy sons' sons.

Do not try to correct other people but correct yourself. We cannot change other people, only ourselves. If you see someone in the church that you think is not a Christian, pray that they will receive God. While in church, keep your focus on worshiping God. Do not look around to see who else is there. Distractions only serve to rob you of time spent worshiping God and in His presents.

Did you know that Satan knows every word in the Bible? He knows who God is and does not doubt. Satan just chooses not to worship God.

Christians are the ones who not only believe but they read the word of God and worship Him. They also obey God's word and conduct themselves according to God's word.

Mathew 7:15 Beware of false prophets, which come to you in sheep's clothing, but inwardly they are ravening wolves.

Yes, there are false prophets in the world and even in the church. Their only purpose is to smile and spread discord among Christians. When that happens, Satan is at his happiest. Do not spread a word of gossip and do not listen to gossip. The old saying is that a dog that will bring a bone, will also take one. This means that someone who brings gossip will gossip about you too.

2 Samuel 22:50 Therefore I will give thanks unto thee, O Lord, among the heathen, and I will sing praises unto your name.

Psalms 18:49 Therefore will I give thanks unto you, O Lord, among the heathen, and sing praises unto your name.

Psalms 22:3 But You are holy, O thou that inhabits the praises of Israel.

If you keep your mind on God, He will keep His mind on you. God will smile when you are singing His praises. God inhabits the praises and worship of His people.

Psalms 9:10 And they that know your name will put their trust in you: for you, Lord, have not forsaken them that seek you.

1 Thessalonians 5:17 Pray without ceasing.

Do not wait until you are in church to worship and praise God. Worship Him without ceasing (stopping). How can you do that? As you get closer to God, He will get closer to you. You will be doing something and suddenly you realize that you have been humming a Christian song of praise. It grows on you, and it feels so good.

If you are not looking for the good things of God, you will not see them. You will simply allow science to explain a miracle away. If you allow science to explain a miracle away, God does not receive the glory and you will not receive your next miracle.

I have shared with you things that can increase happiness in your life. I hope you have been listening. As the old saying goes, "You can lead a horse to water, but you can't make him drink." I can tell you the facts as I know them, but I cannot make you believe them. The choice/decision is yours my friend.

At times I have thought of how difficult this life is. We struggle through birth and every day thereafter. We do not stop struggling until after we leave this life. If life is this difficult with God on our side, how are all the other people getting through life without knowing Him?

This life is a test. It is a test to see who we will choose, God or something else. It is also a test to see how we will manage our problems. Will you call upon God for your help or rely on our own feeble strengths? Will you live your life for God or for yourself? The choices are yours and yours alone. Choose wisely, my friend.

Isiah 41:10 Fear thou not; for I am with you: be not dismayed; for I am your God: I will strengthen you; yes, I will help you; yes, I will uphold you with the right hand of my righteousness. Mirror Him

Bank Slide

Numbers 6:24-25 The Lord bless you and keep you: The Lord make his face shine upon you and be gracious unto you.

It was just another one of those hot summer days in Florida. Even the shade of the old oak tree felt like a sauna. The Florida sandspurs were looking for water. On days like this, the only thing to do was go swimming. You had your choice of a swimming pool, the beach, a river or one of the lakes. We did not have a swimming pool; the beach was too hot so that left a lake or river.

On this day, we all headed to a lake. We had decided not only to go swimming but to do a little water skiing as well. Although I had lived in Florida most of my life, I had never gone water skiing. I do not know why I had never tried it, I just never had. But this day, I was to give it my best try.

Before long, it was my turn to water ski. In the boat were my wife's brother David and his wife. I did not know that David had not pulled a skier prior to this day. I readied myself in the water and gave him a signal to shove the boat's throttle forward. The boat accelerated and within a moment or two, I was up and water skiing.

We circled the lake once and then twice before I gave him the signal to take me in. David steered the boat towards the sandy shore. As he came within two hundred feet of the shore, he turned to the bow of the boat towards the middle of the lake. I released the towrope and quickly realized that he had not brought me in close enough to the shore. It was either that or I did not swing across the back of the boat fast enough. I had to swim for what seemed to be a long way to the shore. When I was able to touch the bottom of the lake, I could feel mussels and sticks.

Before long it was my turn once again to water ski. This time up, my sister Betsy and her husband were in the boat. Her husband had pulled skiers many times before. I readied myself, gave the signal and I was up and away. After a couple of trips around the lake, I gave him the signal to take me to the shore.

Her husband was a speedster at heart. As he headed to the shoreline, he never slowed the boat. In my mind, I was remembering my wife's brother pulling me. So, I swung as far to my left as I could. I was hoping to come across the back of the boat with enough speed that I would not have to swim for the shore like before.

Dale never let up on the throttle as he came in closer to the shore than David had. He turned the steering wheel sharply as he turned the boat towards deeper water.

I, moments before had begun crossing behind the boat. As I turned loose of the towrope, I began hearing a strange buzzing sound. I quickly realized that it was the sound of water buzzing from under my water skies. I was now racing towards the shore at high speed.

My mind was now racing as thoughts raced through my head. I thought, "Should I drop down in the water and swim for it"? What if those sticks and mussels on the bottom cut me? Then I thought, I have seen them do it on TV. I will remain on my skies and just before I reach shore, I will jump out of my skis and jog to a stop".

It was a good plan, but...as I looked towards the shoreline, I saw the crowd of people that were my family. They were parting in the middle and running in opposite directions. They looked like the Red Sea that the Bible speaks of. God parted it so Moses and his people could cross on dry ground.

Everything seemed to be in slow motion now. There was the shoreline just ahead. As I approached at a high rate of speed, I jumped in an effort to escape from my water skies. The skies made contact with the wet dirt and stopped instantly. The rubber boot on the skies grabbed my toes and I was now in a free-fall. I landed on my stomach in the wet dirt and slid ten feet or so before coming to a stop.

When I finally stopped sliding, I quickly stood up to check my body for damage. My chest was very pink, and my stomach was almost cherry red but there was no blood. Yep, with everything still intact, it was a good day. You know what they say, "Even a crash landing is a good landing if you can walk away from it."

I looked at the ground and there was a wide skid mark in the wet dirt where my chest and stomach had slid. It looked like an alligator had slid out of the river and onto the bank.

It was only then that I realized that I was not alone. While everyone had run away from the point of my crash landing, there was one man who did not move. He simply stood there watching the entire event unfold. I had slid right in front of him as he stood motionless watching. This man was older than I with gray, almost white hair. He wore sandals, light blue shorts, a brightly colored Hawaiian shirt, sunglasses, and a straw hat.

As I surveyed my body for damage, he too was looking for blood. I looked up into his sunglasses and very calmly, without even a crack of a smile he stated, "Now that is the funniest thing, I have seen all day". With that and still not a crack of a smile, he just turned and walked away.

Within seconds, everyone in our group came over to ask if I was injured. I was none the worse for the shore slide. I gave God praise that nothing was broken, and nothing was bleeding. That is one incident that could have ended with all sorts of things broken. I did decide to hang up the skis and not tempt God for the remainder of the day.

God is so good. He watches over us when our heads are in the clouds, and we do not have our minds on what we are doing. All He asks in return is for us to love Him and give Him the glory and praise for what He has done for us.

Do not forget to tell others what God has done for you. Thank Him for a good night's sleep. Thank Him for the food you have to eat and the air that you have to breathe. Those are the basic things. There are numerous things that we should acknowledge. Give Him thanks for all those things as well. Then, give Him thanks for everything again. The things that did not go right, cause a person to call on Him for His help. Draw close to Him and He will draw close to you.

Without the challenges of life, most of us would not thank God enough. We would go about our daily lives as though a great day was normal. It would not be long before we would become complacent in our worshiping God. After that comes a falling away from Him. Soon, we would scarcely give Him a single thought. We would think that we were the governors of our lives and not God. Very soon, we would become lost, without God and without hope.

My prayer for you is that you never lose sight of God's love for you, no matter what your circumstances. Always be looking for God's blessings and give Him thanks for all things.

Romans 8:28 And we know that all things work together for good of them that love God, to them who are the called according to his purpose.

Psalms 145:20 The LORD preserves all them that love him: but all the wicked will he destroy. *Mirror Him*

The Visitation

Psalms 150:6 Let everything that has breath praise the LORD. Praise you the LORD.

Years ago, my job while working for a large electrical utility company was to analyze the electrical usage of our largest customers. Due to equipment issues, we had fallen behind on our workload. On this Saturday morning, I had arrived at work at my usual time to catch up on work. I usually did not work on weekends or alone.

Our office was located in a, not-so-good part of town. As you pull up to the intersection just one block from our office, you could see a bullet hole in the lighted street sign. Frequently, one could step into our parking lot and observe drug dealers selling on the opposite corner. On occasions, cars had been broken into in our parking lot during the day.

Soon, an electric security gate was installed along with a security system for our building. Although there were security systems and cameras installed, it only slowed the theft and vandalism.

I arrived at work, enter the gate, park in my usual space, unlock the door, and turned the security system off. I went throughout the building just to make sure everything was locked and secure before I continued to my office. Once there, I settled in to begin work.

Everything was normal for the first couple of hours and then it began. I was the only one scheduled to be in the entire building that Saturday. But I felt as though I was not alone. I again rose from my seat and left my office to survey the interior of the building yet again. The building was all clear and I was the only one in the building. The doors were still locked up tight and secure.

I began working once again and the feeling persisted. You know you get the feeling that someone is watching you. Not just watching you but staring intently at you. Each time I would look around, there was no one there. So, I began to say a prayer and reminded the Lord of His promise. I said, "Lord, you said you would give your angels charge over us so we would not stumble." "Lord, you said that a thousand could fall on our left and ten thousand could fall on our right, but harm would not come close to us".

Psalms 91:7 A thousand shall fall at your side, and ten thousand at your right hand; but it shall not come near you.

Psalms 91:11-12** **For He shall give His angels charge over you, to keep you in all your ways. They shall lift you up in their hands, lest you dash your foot against a stone.

Luke 4:10 For it is written, He shall give his angels charge over you, to keep you:

Luke 4:11 And in their hands they shall lift you up, lest at any time you dash your foot against a stone.

Although I had faith that God would protect me, I was still very uneasy. After several more minutes, the feeling grew much stronger. It was like whoever was watching me was much, much closer now. I could feel their presence behind me getting closer as each second passed. I could almost feel their breath on the back of my neck.

It was then that I decided to jerk my head around to see who was there and confront them face to face. As I jerked my head around, I saw nothing. I could only smell whoever was there. I know that sounds strange, but it is the absolute truth.

There was a gentle fragrance that filled my office. It was soft and sweet, yet it smelled incredibly old. Later, I would describe this fragrance to someone as an old Victorian scent.

The fragrance lingered for several minutes as I sat there at my desk looking around. All too soon, it was gone and with it was the feeling of being watched. Was this an angel sent to watch over me? Was it my guardian angel sent to protect me? Did the angle get too close and reveal its presents? Did the angle reveal too much? Was it there to reassure me that God had my back?

2 Kings 6:14 Therefore sent he thither horses, and chariots, and a great host: and they came by night, and surrounded the city about.

2 Kings 6:15 And when the servant of the man of God (Elisha) ***was risen early, and gone forth, behold, a host*** (enemy) ***surrounded the city both with horses and chariots. And his servant said unto him, alas, my master, what shall we do?***

2 Kings 6:16 And he answered, Fear not: for they that are with us are more than they that are with them.

2 Kings 6:17 And Elisha prayed, and said, LORD, I pray thee, open his eyes, that he may see. And the LORD opened the eyes of the young man; and he saw: and behold, the mountain was full of

horses and chariots of fire round about Elisha.

There are many things of God that we do not understand and are unable to comprehend. Someday when we get to heaven, we will be able to sit with our Lord and receive all these answers. Until that day, we must keep our faith that God has our best interests at heart. We must trust Him with our whole hearts. We should worship and give Him praise and thanks for everything without ceasing.

Keep your faith in God no matter how the circumstances may appear to be. God always knows what is going on and is always in control. Always remember, when things seem the most hopeless, place your faith and hope in God. He will always come shining through. Perhaps not the way that you thought He would work it out but He will always complete what He starts.

Psalms 69:34 Let the heaven and earth praise Him, the seas, and everything that moves therein.

Psalms 104:33 I will sing unto the LORD as long as I live: I will sing praise to my God while I have my being.

Psalms 111:1 Praise ye the LORD. I will praise the LORD with my whole heart,

in the assembly of the upright, and in the congregation.

Psalms 119:164 Seven times a day do I praise you because of your righteous judgments.

John 3:16 says, "For God so loved the world (you and me) that He gave His only begotten son so that whosoever believed on Him (Jesus Christ) could have everlasting life. He that believeth on him is not condemned: but he that believeth not is condemned already because he hath not believed in the name of the only begotten Son of God." *Mirror Him*

The Timekeeper

Psalms 27:5 For in the time of trouble He shall hide me in His pavilion: in the secret of His tabernacle shall He hide me; He shall set me up upon a rock.

Ecclesiastes 3:1-8 To everything there is a season, and a time to every purpose under the heaven: A time to be born, and a time to die; a time to plant, and a time to pluck up that which is planted; A time to kill, and a time to heal; a time to break down, and a time to build up; A time to weep, and a time to laugh; a time to mourn, and a time to dance; A time to cast away stones, and a time to gather stones together; a time to embrace, and a time to refrain from embracing; A time to get, and a time to lose; a time to keep, and a time to cast away; A time to rend, and a time to sew; a time to keep silence, and a time to speak; A time to love, and a time to hate; a time of war, and a time of peace.

As we travel through this life, we seldom know what influence we have upon someone else. It would be wonderful if everyone shared God's love with someone else. Wouldn't it be splendid if everyone performed random acts of kindness? Random acts of kindness is when someone does something good or nice for someone else. We perform random acts of kindness without seeking rewards or thanks from other people. We perform random acts of kindness without telling someone else what we have done. God, Himself will reward us in heaven soon for our good deeds.

God rewards us for such things as these. By making a practice of doing such things, we are building up our rewards in heaven. That is unless we are doing it for recognition while still on earth. If that is the reason for doing these things, we will receive our reward here on earth. I would rather receive my rewards in heaven, how about you?

Matthew 6:19 Lay not up for yourselves treasures upon earth, where moth and rust doth corrupt, and where thieves break through and steal:

Matthew 6:20 But lay up for yourselves treasures in heaven, where neither moth nor rust doth corrupt, and where thieves do not break through nor steal:

Recently my wife and I went through a drive-thru for a quick snack. We placed our order at one of the two speakers at the drive-through. As we pulled forward to the pay window, we were greeted by an employee who worked there. The employee said, "Your order has been paid for". I asked, "Excuse me"? The young man said, "The lady in the car ahead of you paid for your order".

My wife and I tried our best to figure out who the lady was but could not. We wanted to thank her but could not as she drove away quickly. We never knew who that lady was and still do not know to this very day. As we watched her car pull away, we simply said, "God, please bless that lady whoever she is for her random act of kindness".

I do not believe that God wanted us to thank the lady. I believe God wanted not only to bless us but to bless her as well. For if we perform random acts of kindness, we feel good within ourselves. At the same time, it makes other people feel good as well. We also add to our bank account in heaven. If we had been able to thank her, she would have received her reward here on earth. We would have cheated her out of a heavenly reward.

We had the money to pay for our order but the thought of a random act of kindness made our day go better. We had done the same thing for other people but had never been on the receiving end. It made us feel good to be able to do it for someone else. Now, someone was doing it for us. Won't you join us in performing random acts of kindness? It will make your day much better to do something special for someone else. It will also make their day much better to think that someone cared.

As we perform a random act of kindness, please do not forget to say a prayer for that person. Yes, it is nice to help someone feel better for a moment or a day. But the one who makes us feel better forever is God. He alone is the creator of all things and that includes good blessings. He can help a person feel better even when we cannot. All good things come from God, so do not forget to daily ask Him to bless someone else.

Always let your Godly light shine. Let others see God's presence in you. Be kind, be patient, and be quick with a good word for God. Be quick with a helping hand. Be ever so slow to anger. Love God with all your heart and seek Him every moment of every day. Always look for the blessings of God as it would be such a shame to not notice one. Tell others of the blessings that God has bestowed upon you so they will know of His love.

2 Timothy 4:2 Preach the word; be instant in season, out of season; reprove, rebuke, exhort with all longsuffering and doctrine.

Galatians 5:22-23 But the fruit of the Spirit is love, joy, peace, long-suffering, gentleness, goodness, faith, meekness,

temperance: against such, there is no law.

Ephesians 5:9 For the fruit of the Spirit is in all goodness, righteousness, and truth.

We frequently do not know to what extent our actions affect other people. I heard a story a long time ago about a man who worked in a factory. One of his job duties was to blow a large steam whistle at exactly noon each day.

He always walked to work, as he lived near the factory. The route that he walked took him each day past a jewelry store. Inside the jewelry store, on the wall hung a large clock. In those days everyone believed that jewelry store owners always had the correct time. So, each day he would stop, look at the clock, and set his watch by it.

One day he became curious about where the jeweler got the correct time for his clock. So, on his way home, he stopped and asked the jeweler. The jeweler replied, "Oh that is easy. Every day at exactly noon, the factory blows a large steam whistle.

Each of these men had been obtaining the time from each other for years and never knew it. We will never know all the lives we have touched by our words and our actions. So please make sure that your words and actions reflect God's love.

Matthew 4:19 And Jesus said unto them, follow me, and I will make you fishers of men.

Always let your Godly light shine. Make sure others see God's spirit in you. Live your life as a kind and good example for others. Then when you are old, you will not feel regret about the choices you have made during your life.

Remember, someone is watching and listening to you. You may be unaware of it, but you are setting an example for someone every day of your life. They could be someone that you only slightly know. They may be someone that you love very much. You may be unaware that they are watching, listening, and learning from you. Would you want them to grow up just like you or someone better? Would you want them to make the same mistakes that you have made?

Have you ever noticed the dirt paths crisscrossing a cow pasture? They were made by one cow following another. Each cow had walked that path many times before and they will go out of their way to get to a path. Then they will follow it to wherever it is going. The examples we set for others are similar to these cow trails. Other people could be following our lead. Be a leader and not a follower unless you are following Jesus Christ.

If we do not set a good example for others to follow, it could turn into a generational curse. A grandfather made a bad choice in his life, and the son makes the same mistake, but will the grandson make the same mistake? With God's help, we can break generational curses in our lives. We can escape the path of a not-so-good example, but it takes God's help. It will take effort on your part as well. Remember, it is all about your choices.

Pass along a kind word to everyone you encounter. Give the absolute best advice that you can. Never listen to a rumor or share one with someone else. Never speak an unkind word. Always share a smile. By doing these things, you will be a wonderful example. Always give God the praise and glory for what He is doing in your life. Do not forget to share a word from God with others. These are examples of only a few of the good things we can pass on to others. By doing the good things, heavenly rewards will be yours.

Oh, come on, be truthful with yourself. Everyone has made bad choices and that includes you and me. We have all made choices that we could have made better than we did. Even when we are diligent, we will occasionally make decisions that are not perfect. Keep leaning on God and our decisions will become much better.

We owe it to ourselves to be truthful first with ourselves. If we make a poor choice, do not blame it on others. If we do not admit to ourselves that we were wrong, we cannot correct it. We should not only watch what we say but also how we act. For if we do not, we could be held accountable in the life which is sure to come. Yes, we can also be held accountable for the bad influence that we have had on another person's life.

Job 27:4 My lips shall not speak wickedness, nor my tongue utter deceit.

Philippians 4:8 Finally, brethren, whatsoever things are true, what-so-ever things are honest, whatsoever things are just, whatsoever things are pure, whatsoever things are lovely, whatsoever things are of good report; if there be any virtue, and if there be any praise, think on these things.

Remember, good manners, a kind word, a helping hand, a smile and a word from God will cause people to remember you kindly.

We can change our world for the better if we continually set a godly example for others. A journey begins with the first step. Changing our world for the better begins with one person.

Matthew 15:23 A man hath joy by the answer of his mouth: and a word is spoken in due season, how good is it!

Matthew 15:24 The way of life is above to the wise, that he may depart from hell beneath.

Matthew 15:25 The Lord will destroy the house of the proud: but he will establish the border of the window.

Matthew 15:26 The thoughts of the wicked are an abomination to the Lord: but the words of the pure are pleasant words.

Matthew 15:27 He that is greedy of gain troubles his own house; but he that hates gifts shall live.

Matthew 15:28 The heart of the righteous studies to answer but the mouth of the wicked pours out evil things.

Matthew 15:29 The Lord is far from the wicked: but he hears the prayer of the righteous.

Matthew 15:30 The light of the eyes rejoices the heart: and a good report makes the bones fat.

Matthew 15:31 The ear that hears the reproof of life abides among the wise.

Matthew 15:32 He that refuses instruction despites his own soul: but he that hears reproof (correction) *gets understanding.*

Matthew 15:33 The fear of the Lord is the instruction of wisdom; and before honor is humility.

Mirror Him

Heart Wishes

It happened to me, many years ago while living in a different part of the United States. I had received a telephone call from my dad with news about my mother. Dad wanted to let me know that mom was to undergo surgery the following day. I do not know why dad did not let me know sooner.

I told dad that since I had just started a new job and I was fourteen-hundred miles away, I did not see how I could make it home. We talked for a few minutes more and then we ended the call.

My new job at Kimberly Clark Paper Manufacturing Company caused me to work the midnight shift. Upon getting off work at seven o'clock the next morning, I headed home, took a shower, and went to bed.

I awoke later that day after several hours of sleep. It was now afternoon when I received another phone call from my dad. The first thing he said was, "I thought you said you couldn't make it". I asked, "What are you talking about?" He replied, "Your mom came through the surgery fine, but then you already know that". I asked again, "What are you talking about?" He said, "Your trip down here.

I thought that you would have stayed a little longer". I said, "Ok, now you are starting to worry me. What are you talking about?"

Dad said, "I'll tell you what I am talking about. Your mother came through the surgery fine and was taken to the recovery room. I stayed with her until they took her back to her room. When we entered the room, one of the three lady patients in the room said, "Your son was just in here inquiring about his mother". My dad said, "Not our son"! One of our sons lives out of state and the other one is too young to come up here". At the time, if you were not sixteen years old or older, the first-floor lobby was as far as you were allowed to go.

After dad said that the other ladies verified what the first lady had said. They told dad that a young man had entered the room, stated that he was Larry O'Neal (they called me by name), and wanted to check on his mother's condition.

Dad pulled his wallet out and showed them my picture. The ladies confirmed that they had just seen and spoken with me moments before.

Dad quickly went to the nurse's station which was just across the hall. But before dad could say a single word, the head nurse said,

"Your son was just here asking about his mother". The nurse said, "He just got on the elevator right over there."

The hospital only had two floors. Instead of waiting for the elevator, dad ran down the stairs and beat the elevator to the ground floor. But when the elevator doors opened, he said that there was no one in the elevator. The elevator was completely empty!

All I knew was, that I was very tired when I got off work that morning. I went home, took a shower, and went straight to bed. But God knows the desires of our hearts. I know that Mom and dad would have liked for me to have been there.

Somehow four people saw me and spoke with me. But God's arm is not short. We can pray for someone miles away and God can heal them instantly. I have seen it happen numerous times during my life. In fact, I belong to a prayer group that my sister Betsy started while she lived in Alaska. This prayer group stretches from Alaska to Connecticut to Florida, and through many states in between. No matter what time of day or night if one of us needs prayer, we send a short message to all the others. Within minutes people from all over our country are praying for the same person's healing. Yes, God has answered prayer through this social media network many times.

Mom recovered from her surgery and lived many years after that. God is all-powerful and works in mysterious ways. He knew that hearts were wishing that I could have been there. Perhaps mom had prayed the night before her surgery that somehow God would make a way for me to make the trip.

The only thing that I knew was, I went to sleep and woke up hours later. I had no memory of traveling to that hospital fourteen hundred miles away.

I did and still do have faith in God's miracle-working power. My Bible tells me, what God did when He walked upon this earth, which He is still able to do today.

Hebrews 13:8 Jesus Christ is the same yesterday, today, and forever.

When I had gone to bed, I knew that God had healed members of my family before. I know that God is still in the miracle business today. I knew that godly people were praying for mom. I also knew that she was in God's hands. I hold fast to my faith in God.

John 20:29 Jesus said to him, "Thomas because you have seen Me, you have

believed. Blessed** are **those who have not seen and** yet **have believed."

Our faith is well-founded if we place it in God. It is called faith when we have not seen proof of His greatness and still believe. If we have seen it, it is called proof. God, Himself calls us blessed if we have not seen and still believe His word. *Mirror Him*

Gentle Persuasion

Matthew 24:24 For there shall arise false Christs, and false prophets, and shall show great signs and wonders; insomuch that, if it were possible, they shall deceive the very elect.

Mark 13:5 And Jesus answering them began to say, be careful that no man deceives you:

Why would Jesus say the same thing multiple times in the Bible? Answer: because He thought it was important. If Jesus thought it was important, shouldn't we be listening?

What does **deceive** mean? It means causing someone to believe something that is not true. What does the word **elect** mean in Matthew 24:24 in the scripture above? Elect in that scripture means, the people who are chosen by God, the Christians, those with great bible knowledge, the learned people. So, we have people that can be persuaded to believe something that is obviously not true.

How can the elect people who are supposed to be smart and schooled in the Bible believe something that is false? There is an old saying that says, "If someone hears something often enough, they will begin to believe it". The thinking and beliefs of people are conditioned over time. Over time, people's thoughts and beliefs can be corrupted to believe a lie.

There are people who will believe anything that they see on the internet and on television. I have heard someone say, "You do not know, that person has studied for many years. So, they must know what they are talking about." My thought is, that we have been warned by Jesus Himself to be very cautious of what we see and hear.

Often a preacher is not reading from the bible at all. They are reading from notes that they have compiled. We must guard the facts that we know and the evidence that we have seen. We must place our faith in God, His Son, and the Holy Spirit. All else are the words of man which may not be the truth.

Romans 1:28 ¶And even as they did not like to retain God in their knowledge, God gave them over to a reprobate mind, to do those things which are not convenient.

2 Thessalonians 2:11 And for this cause God shall send them strong delusion, that they should believe a lie:

2 Thessalonians 2:12 That they all might be damned who believed not the

truth but had pleasure in unrighteousness.

People often believe everything that they hear on the news. But some news stations, newspapers, and even websites on the internet have an agenda. As with some sources of information, they will try to entice you to believe things as they see them. Only God and His Holy Word are the sources of all truth.

I have heard people say, "The Bible contradicts itself". That statement my friend is absolutely false. It is only our lack of understanding and knowledge that causes us to perceive it that way. True, there are gaps in the Bible where all of the information, is not included. It is in these instances that we must trust and have faith in God. One day we will be able to sit with God Himself and ask Him to fill in those gaps in our knowledge and understanding.

Hebrews 11:6 But without faith, it is impossible to please Him: for he that comes to God must believe that He is and that He is a rewarder of them that diligently seek Him.

Ecclesiastes 3:11 He hath made everything beautiful in His time: also, He hath set the world in their heart so

that no man can find out the work that God makes from the beginning to the end.

People sometimes think only with their intellect. If they think only with their intellect, they will miss many things of God. God often works in ways that we are not capable of understanding. Intellect does not mean wisdom or understanding.

Romans 11:33 Oh, how great are God's riches, wisdom, and knowledge! How impossible it is for us to understand his decisions and his ways!

1 Peter 1:14 So you must live as God's obedient children. Don't slip back into your old ways of living to satisfy your own desires. You didn't know any better then.

Proverbs 3:5 Trust in the LORD with all your heart; and lean not unto your own understanding.

Some will believe the internet before they believe their own eyes or the word of God. There are people who will lie to themselves to the point that they will believe it as truth. Never lie to yourself. There are already enough people out there eager to lie to you. Place your trust in God.

Matthew 7:15 Beware of false prophets, which come to you in sheep's clothing, but inwardly they are ravening wolves.

Matthew 24:4 And Jesus answered and said unto them, take heed that no man deceives you.

Matthew 24:5 For many shall come in my name, saying, I am Christ; and shall deceive many.

Matthew 24:11 And many false prophets shall rise and shall deceive many.

Once you know the truth, we must hold onto it and passionately guard it. For in the scriptures that you have just read, Jesus said there will be people who will try their absolute best to make you believe a lie. They will say to you that they come to you in the name of our Lord, but they come to deceive. They will cover their true intentions.

Years ago, our neighborhood experienced people walking around wanting to discuss the Bible. Each Saturday, they typically walked from house to house asking a simple question. This question would be about a Bible scripture or something that you believe. You would answer their question. Then they would tell you about their thoughts on why your answer was not correct. Of course, they would elaborate on their thought about that scripture. These folks do not believe that Jesus Christ is the son of God. They were well-dressed and very polite. If you talked with them once, they would be back the following Saturday.

On this Saturday, I was home alone when the doorbell rang. I arrived at my door to see two ladies standing outside. I opened the door and asked politely, "May I help you"? One of the ladies introduced herself and the other lady and then she asked a question. She asked, "Where do you believe Heaven is"? I replied, "I don't care where Heaven is, just as long as when I die, I go to be where my God is". The first lady looked puzzled at the second lady, then she said, "Thank you, have a nice day". Then, both ladies walked away.

The following Saturday, one of the ladies showed up at my front door again. This time she had a different lady with her. When I answered the door, she introduced the second lady as her supervisor. She said, "I did not understand your answer last Saturday". Then she asked the same question again, "Where do you believe Heaven is"? I replied as before, "I don't care where Heaven is, just as long as when I die, I go to be where my God is". Both ladies looked puzzled at each other and said, "Have a nice day" and walked away.

That occurred about forty years ago and to this day I now see them on Saturdays. The difference is, that each time they walk past our house, they look our way but never step foot in our yard. It is very strange and like our house has an invisible mark on it.

When you have seen the miracles of God, within your own family as I have, I know that what I believe is correct. Therefore, I will not allow anyone to alter my beliefs. Once we have seen the proof, we must be ever so careful to guard the truth. We must be cautious as to what we allow ourselves to hear and see from others.

John 20:29 Jesus saith unto him, Thomas, because thou hast seen me, thou hast believed: blessed are they that have not seen, and yet have believed.

Whether we are sitting in church or watching preaching on the television, we should have our Bible open. We should be able to verify what we are hearing, through our own Holy Bible. If our Bible does not verify what we are hearing, turn your hearing off and remove yourself. Read the scriptures before and after the scripture that is being discussed to understand the context of it. Ask the Holy Spirit to help your understanding. Remember that there are wolves in sheep's clothing everywhere. Satan is very subtle, changing a word here and a word there over time. Then before we know it, we have drifted from the path that God intended for us, and we believe a lie. Be Very Cautious!

I am aware that I have said it before, but it bears repeating. Remember to read only a bible that has the word ***begotten*** in **John 3:16**. Why? Because if it does not have the word ***begotten*** in that verse, it is a counterfeit bible with things altered. These altered things could place your feet on a path to soul destruction.

Why would a bible be a counterfeit if the word ***begotten*** is not in John 3:16? Because that one word denotes bloodline. Without that one word in the Bible, God's bloodline or DNA has been removed. This would make Jesus Christ just another human being and not God's only ***begotten*** son. If that were the case, we would have no hope of being forgiven of our sins. We could ask each other for the forgiveness of our sins, but we would still have the sin stains upon our souls.

God has many spiritual sons and daughters but only one **begotten** son. After we have confessed our sins and asked Jesus Christ to be our Lord and Savior, we become the children of God. At that time, we are adopted into the family of God.

John 14:6 Jesus saith unto him, I am the way, the truth, and the life: no man cometh unto the Father, but by me.

Then there is the question if someone was going to change that, what other things in the bible did they change? You know, they did change other things to mislead us on purpose. Were they inspired by Satan to do such a thing?

Genesis 3:1 Now the serpent was more subtle than any beast of the field which the LORD God had made. And he said unto the woman, Yea, hath God said, you shall not eat of every tree of the garden?

Genesis 3:2 And the woman said unto the serpent, we may eat of the fruit of the trees of the garden:

Genesis 3:3 But of the fruit of the tree, which is in the midst of the garden, God hath said, We shall not eat of it, neither shall we touch it, lest we die.

Genesis 3:4 And the serpent said unto the woman, you shall not surely die:

Genesis 3:5 For God doth know that in the day you eat thereof, then your eyes shall be opened, and you shall be as gods, knowing good and evil.

Satan was speaking of physical death when he was deceiving Eve in the garden. God was speaking of spiritual death. That is why the Bible speaks of being born again. It is speaking of a spiritual rebirth back into the family of God.

I have heard people say, "One of the altered bibles is easier to read." To which I say, "You may be better off reading the book, Moby Dick". It will do your soul just as much good. The book, Moby Dick should not damage your soul. Yes, people are changing the word of God, so be extremely cautious.

I had heard of a man who was very versed in reading ancient written works. He traveled to Israel many years ago. While visiting a museum, he saw an ancient scroll displayed behind a glass enclosure. As he began to read the scroll, he recognized the writing being from the book of Isaiah in his own Bible. I find it very comforting to know that those scrolls were translated with such accuracy, with nothing changed or altered. That is something that I can rely upon to feed and guide my soul. In today's world, that assurance is something precious and rare indeed.

Revelation 22:18 For I testify unto every man that hears the words of the prophecy of this book. If any man shall add unto these things, God shall add unto him the plagues that are written in this book:

Revelation 22:19 And if any man shall take away from the words of the book of this prophecy, God shall take away his part out of the book of life, and out of the holy city, and from the things which are written in this book.

Yes, this is an especially important chapter. Your very soul is at stake as well as your eternal home. Now you have been **Warned**! Do not take any chances with something that is of such importance. Trust and have faith in God. He will never mislead or betray your confidence. *Mirror Him*

Artificial Intelligence

Some of the following may seem like science fiction, but I can assure you that it is something that we should consider. Many things that we once thought were science fiction are now a reality. We need to read the following with an open mind to the possibilities of things, soon to be a reality.

The buzz all over the world today is Artificial Intelligence or AI for short. We have devices all around us that use AI. Most of these devices are being taken for granted and never noticed in our daily lives. They say AI will make life better for us. Remember, sugar tastes good but it can be harmful.

We have devices that tell us the time, allow us to read our mail, research things, tell us what day it is, give us directions, calls a friend, track appointments, and see friends face to face. We have devices that tell us when to go to sleep and when to wake up. There are even refrigerators that will create a shopping list for you. At a touch, the refrigerator door will appear as transparent glass so that you can see the contents inside. There are small devices that when spoken to will change the channel you are watching on TV. You can ask the same device a question and it will usually answer you with the correct answer. There are even cars and trains that now drive themselves without human intervention. Yet we do not see what is right in front of our faces.

We use AI to make our lives easier but at the same time, it is making us weaker. We are relying on it to the extent that it has begun to affect our very reasoning. Years ago, one had to remember phone numbers or write them down. The telephone companies published a book with everyone's name and phone number listed inside. This book was called a phone book. Imagine that!

Nowadays you do not need to remember. Pick up your cell phone and you can look up someone's phone number. This same device will give you turn by turn to your destination. You can stay connected with your friends or just play games. Have I missed anything?

Some people simply could not survive without their electronic connections. Some people have no opinion of their own anymore. That is until they consult the internet to see what it says about the subject at hand. In fact, in some cases, it would appear that some people no longer use their brains at all. For those people, their god has become the internet and or social media.

I have often told others that our brain is like a muscle. The more you use it, the stronger it gets. Stop using a muscle and it turns to flab. Stop using your brain and it will turn into mush. Stop feeding a brain Godly things, and it will turn to evil things. Turning to evil things is human nature. That is why we must be born again into the family of God. That is why we must be vigilant about the things we see and hear.

Philippians 4:8 Finally, brethren, whatever things are true, whatever things are noble, whatever things are just, whatever things are pure, whatever things are lovely, whatever things are of good report if there is any virtue and if there is anything praiseworthy, meditate on these things.

1 Timothy 4:15 Meditate on these things; give yourself entirely to them, that your progress may be evident to all.

So, AI is a good thing up to a point you say? Do you have any idea where that point is? Do you know where AI is heading? We must ask ourselves; do the people promoting AI have an agenda? Who knows and who cares maybe your answer? You may say, "If it makes life easier for me, it will be worth it"? What about your children and their children that will follow you? Could our enemy Satan use this as a tool against them? The answer to that is yes.

Have you ever wondered where all of this is heading? If you have ever wondered about this, read your Bible. Yes, the Bible tells you where humanity and AI is heading. But you say, "It can't be"! If you wait to see for sure where it is going, it will be too late when we arrive. The only thing one needs to do is, read the Bible and watch the daily news. The real news and not a news source with an agenda. The fake news will lead you to believe that all is well with the world, meanwhile, it is a train wreck just waiting to happen.

Yes, little Timmy, some news sources today have an agenda. That means that they will exaggerate and lie to you, so you will see things their way. Why haven't we ever heard of the bones of giants that have been discovered? Answer: Authorities in high places do not want you to know that once real giants roamed the earth. These giants did all sorts of despicable things to humans. These giants were not of human origin. Why would they not want you to know that? Because if you knew that the giants mentioned in the Bible were real, you may start believing other things contained in the Bible are true as well. They do not want you to believe anything contained in the Bible. Finding the bones of these giants would be proof that the Bible tells of one more truth. Pile one biblical truth upon another and soon you will believe the entire Bible.

Some people who create fake news want you to think that they are smarter than they really are. Some scientists are in this same category. Some people are looking for more fame, wealth, and power. Be careful my friend what you watch and listen to.

They have now created robots that talk, run, and do other human things. There are robots that can answer almost any question that you ask. These robots arrive at their answer based on what the internet has to say about the question at hand. How truthful is the information on the internet? Surely everything on the internet is the truth, right? Surely there is no misinformation on the internet, right? ***Fact:*** All information on the internet is only as truthful as the people who put it there.

I have often thought it such a waste when someone with broad knowledge dies. It was a human life that has ended. They spent their entire life acquiring knowledge and life lessons. Then, unless they have shared it with others, all that knowledge dies with them. Wouldn't it be wonderful to somehow capture all that knowledge?

But what if we could capture all that knowledge and put it to use? There are engineers and sci working day and night trying to do just that. They are trying to build a machine that can scan the essence of their brain. Then upload all that information into a computer. They have the idea that they can build robots, download their information into a robot and live forever.

What a blinded world we currently live in. These scientists have completely forgotten about a human's spirit and soul. The spirit and soul are two-thirds of what makes up a person. Without the spirit and soul, all one has is knowledge and that is not a human but a shadow of a replacement.

They are now creating robots that will perform (as they put it) all wifely duties. They are working tirelessly to make them as near lifelike as possible.

I have also read that scientists have installed computer chips in animals' brains to control them. I've read that their next step will involve humans. Scientists are talking about installing computer chips containing expanded information into people to extend their knowledge.

So where is all this heading? An article that appeared in www.Dailymail.com dated Dec. 19, 2017, says **Robots and humans will have 'BABIES'** and create a new hybrid species in the next one hundred years, claims an expert.

In the article, Dr. David Levy, author of Love and Sex with Robots, suggests that a computer chip could be used to inject robot genetic code into skin cells. Since when does a robot have a genetic code? Where did this robotic genetic code come from? I have only heard the term genetic code used when someone speaks of living tissue.

AI robots could soon be having 'children' with their owners, according to a leading artificial intelligence expert. They say this will be possible with the recent progress in stem cell research and artificial chromosomes. Are you concerned yet? Where do "stem cells" come from? www.medicalnewstoday.com says: Stem cells originate from living tissues such as embryos. Scientists are also working on ways to develop stem cells from other cells, using genetic "reprogramming" techniques.

So "stem cells" come from living tissue and embryos. What are embryos? Answer:

Tissue from unborn babies or baby parts. Are you beginning to wake up and be concerned?

The Wall Street Journal printed on Sept. 13, 2019, an article By Michael S.A. Graziano: The article says, imagine a future in which a machine can scan your brain and migrate the essentials of your mind to a computer. This is known as mind uploading, preserving a person's consciousness in a digital afterlife. Doesn't that sound a little like playing God? What about the human spirit and soul?

On January 11, 2019, PCMAG.COM had an article By S.C. Stuart that told of a new movie called Replicas. In this movie, actor Keanu Reeves uploaded the consciousness of several of his family members after a horrific car accident. He did this by trying to bring them back to life. Are you alarmed yet? Yes, it is now in the movies training our children.

Look to the past fifty or so years of the movie industry. You will find that motion pictures we have been watching, have played a significant role in our future. They shape and mold what we will accept and what we will not accept.

When I was a child, comic books were a grandiose thing. Do you remember the comic book series "Dick Tracy"? He had a radio wristwatch. It not only told time, but he could communicate with other people with it. We enjoyed the wild imaginations of the writers of those comic books back in the day. Now our reality is that we can have one of those watches just like Dick Tracy. The only thing is, now our watches will do much more than Dick Tracy's could. If Dick Tracy only knew, he would turn green with envy.

The motion picture industry has often pushed the envelope and laid the groundwork for real changes in our society. Do you remember the movie "The Matrix"? Humans are connected to a system that used their bodies to create an electrical grid. Their bodies were generating electricity for use by others. All the while, their minds lived a fantasy existence which was their reality. So, do the motion pictures that we watch create advancements in humanity? Does watching these things plant a seed in the minds of men for these changes or is it another force that is not benevolent (peaceful)?

By now you must be thinking, are those people playing God. If you are not thinking that by now, perhaps you should be. I have witnessed firsthand many miracles of God.

Therefore, I will never doubt anything contained within my Holy Bible. What it tells me is that every time someone tries to play God, something horrifying happens. It never works out like man thought it would. Everything that man has ever created for good, has been used for evil one way or another.

Genesis 1:26 And God said, let Us make man in our image, after our likeness: and let them have dominion over the fish of the sea, and over the fowl of the air, and over the cattle, and over all the earth, and over every creeping thing that creeps upon the earth.

Genesis 1:27 So God created man in His own image, in the image of God created He him, male and female created He them.

So, God created man in His own image. How did that work out for God? Man has turned his back on God. Man has lied to and killed men. Man has devised means and ways to dishonor and disobey God. That was not what God created man for. God sent Jesus Christ to save man, so man would have a way back to God. What will man have to sacrifice to save himself? News Flash: man cannot save himself.

Ecclesiastes 12:13 Let us hear the conclusion of the whole matter: Fear God and keep his commandments: for this is *the whole* duty *of man.*

Matthew 10:28 And fear, not them which kill the body but are not able to kill the soul: but rather fear him which is able to destroy both soul and body in hell.

Man is creating AI robots in his own image. What happens after that? Man has given robots AI intelligence. AI is intelligence without a conscience, love, or any other emotions. Scientists code safeguards into each robot to confine them within certain parameters. In other words, so they will not hurt or kill humans but serve us instead. Didn't God do the same thing? God gave humans rules to live by, but did we? God also gave man a conscience to assist him in knowing right from wrong. Does man use that conscience to govern himself according to God's word? Do men kill men today? Why do men think AI robots will be any different than men themselves?

Exodus 20:13 Thou shalt not kill.

One of God's commandments was, "Thou shall not kill." How many people are killed daily by another person? How many people have died in wars and conflicts? Thousands of humans are being killed daily in abortion clinics across our country. Men are also giving robots those same safeguards. Will robots take heed? Will they listen to that word? Did humans listen to God's commandments? There are robots given the command to kill humans. The militaries all over the world are trying to create the super-soldier. What happens if that gets out of hand? Did you see the movie, "I Robot"? I believe it is one of the must-watch movies.

Genesis 4:8 And Cain talked with Abel his brother: and it came to pass, when they were in the field, that Cain rose up against Abel his brother, and slew him.

But Cain was jealous of Abel because God accepted Abel's offering and not his. So why did God accept Abel's offering and not Cain's? Because God required a blood sacrifice and nothing else will do. Cain was a tiller of the ground, a farmer if you will. Cain offered a part of his harvest as a sin sacrifice to God.

Hebrews 11:4 By faith Able offered unto God a more excellent sacrifice than Cain, by which he obtained witness that he was righteous, God testifying of his

gifts: and by it he being dead yet speaks.

For a long time, I did not fully understand why God accepted Abel's sacrifice and not Cain's. I did not understand why God required a blood sacrifice to cover sins. Then I connected the dots.

Genesis 33:21 Unto Adam also and to his wife did the LORD God make coats of skins and clothed them.

God had shed the first blood to cover sin. He slew two animals in the Garden of Eden to cover Adam and Eve's sins. Adam and Eve had eaten from the forbidden tree of knowledge. They did not know what evil was. They ate from the tree and their spiritual eyes were opened. At that instant, Adam and Eve died a spiritual death because they disobeyed God. Then they saw that they were naked and were ashamed. Then, they hid themselves from God.

Genesis 3:7 And the eyes of them both were opened, and they knew that they were naked, and they sewed fig leaves together and made themselves aprons.

Genesis 3:8 And they heard the voice of the LORD God walking in the garden in the cool of the day (night or early morning)***:***

and Adam and his wife hid themselves from the presence of the LORD God among the trees of the garden.

Genesis 3:9 And the LORD God called unto Adam, and said unto him, "Where are you?"

Genesis 3:10 And he said, I heard your voice in the garden, and I was afraid because I was naked, and I hid myself.

Genesis 3:21 Unto Adam also and to his wife did the Lord God make coats of skins and clothed them.

The skins that covered Adam and Eve's sin came from animals. This was a foreshadowing of things to come, the ultimate sacrifice that would cover our sins. The practice of shedding blood to cover sins continued in the Bible until the crucifixion of Jesus Christ. It is only by the shedding of His blood that our sins were and are forgiven. No other sacrifice will wipe away our sins.

The Bible tells of God's only **begotten** son Jesus Christ who was sacrificed for the sins of the world. This sacrifice would be the last of the blood sacrifices. This one final sacrifice would be enough for all time. With His freely given life's blood, he covered the sins of all who would accept Him as their Lord and Savior. Have you accepted His sacrifice for your sins?

Now man is creating something in his own image. God created something from nothing. Man cannot create the materials they are using to create robots. If you are not God, one can only use substances that are already created and rearrange them into something else.

But man with his limited knowledge remains stiff-necked and defiant towards God. Not only is man attempting to create something in his own image but creating it to stand beside man and to eventually replace God's man.

Have you been aware of these things happening? Did you know that today there are robots for sale on the internet that have been created for the purpose of having sex with a human? It is only a few steps away from robots having babies.

Does that sound too far-fetched for you to believe? Search Google for **TEST TUBE BABY** and you will find a story from 1978. A couple in England could not conceive children. The doctors retrieved one of the eggs from the woman, introduced the counterpart from her husband, and placed it into a laboratory dish.

When the egg from the wife became fertile, they introduced it into the woman's uterus. On July 24, 1978, Louise Joy Brown became the first baby conceived via Vitro Fertilization. She weighed five pounds, twelve ounces at birth, and was delivered by cesarean section.

If you were to search www.google.com for **Artificial Wombs,** you will find the website www.theguardian.com. There it talks about researchers who have created a device that could revolutionize care for babies born extremely premature. This article also shows pictures of the process.

This device has only been tested on premature sheep thus far. In this situation, an extremely premature lamb is placed inside of a plastic bag. It looks like a large sandwich bag. The bag is filled with a substitute similar to amniotic fluid. The fluid is then circulated through a machine that oxygenates and adds nutrients to the lamb's embryo. When the lamb has fully developed and can sustain life on its own, they remove the lamb from the bag.

Can you see where all of this is heading? The article said that they have only tried the artificial womb on lambs. We will never know when they begin trying it on humans until they have been successful.

The next step will be earth-shaking. That next step could be when they announce that they have created a robot that can carry a baby full term and then give birth. Are you ready for that next step? Can you imagine that? At that time, a robot could become a surrogate mother.

Suppose for a minute, you and your spouse could not conceive a child. You could enlist the help of one of the doctors. The doctor could fertilize an egg from the woman and the counterpart from her husband. After two or three weeks, the fertilized egg now an embryo, could be placed in a see-through plastic bag. This artificial womb would be connected to a support system inside of a robot. At any time, you could request the robot to lift her blouse slightly. This would allow you to view your baby's progressing development. Imagine that, no sonogram, no guessing just direct sight.

But then, what happens if you do not like the color of your unborn baby's hair? Will there be an option for them to introduce something in the embryonic fluid to change its hair color? What if you want the baby to have blue instead of green eyes? Will you have the choice to change that as well? With all the genetic studies going on, will you be able to change the gender as well? All of this reminds me of the song, "**In The Year 2525**". Search for it on www.Youtube.com. Zager and Evans recorded the song. I have included the web link, so you do not even have to search for it:

https://www.youtube.com/watch?v=izQB2-Kmiic

This song was written in 1964 and released in 1969. If they were contemplating such things in 1964, what have they achieved? What are they contemplating now? Oh wait, I know part of the answer to that.... robots having babies.

Does all of this seem like science fiction to you? When I was a youth, it seemed like science fiction to us when Dick Tracy communicated through his wristwatch. It seemed like science fiction when people dreamed of color television. It seemed like science fiction years ago when people spoke of sending men to the moon. Nowadays, men are making plans to go to mars. Do not be too quick to dismiss the dreams of men as purely science fiction. A host of advancements have come from the dreams of men and from what we call science fiction. But sometimes man's dreams have resulted in nightmares.

Suggestion: Become a child of God, stay prayed up, and place your faith in Him.

Yes, the future could be a rough ride indeed. But rest assured that God knows what is on the horizon and He has it all under control. The big question is how much more will God allow to happen before He says enough is enough? How soon before He returns to gather His children? Will I be ready for His return? Will you be ready?

You may be saying, Our God is so loving, that He would never send anyone to a place like hell. He is also very intolerant of sin. This means that He and sin cannot be in the same place at the same time. It is like walking into a dark room and turning on a light. God is light and sin is darkness.

Although God would never send anyone to a place like hell, He gives us a choice as to where we will spend our eternal life. We ourselves choose to either accept His sin offering (Jesus Christ) or we choose not to believe Him. By asking Jesus Christ to be our Lord and Savior and living our lives for God, we choose heaven. By not choosing Jesus Christ and not living for God, we choose hell as our eternal home. It is your choice, which will you choose? There is no third option!

John 10:9 I am the door: by me, if any man enter in, he shall be saved, and shall go in and out, and find pasture

John 14:6 Jesus saith unto him, I am the way, the truth, and the life: no man cometh unto the Father, but by me.

Some consider fake news disturbing. Others, find the warnings of the Bible also disturbing. This group of people are not living totally by the Bible. They are on the borderline. They believe what the Bible says, but do not live by it.

The Bible tells of the numerous rewards for living a holy life before God. It reassures us that God loves us deeply and He is a rewarder of those who diligently seek Him. But the choice is yours, rewards or something else.

Hebrews 11:6 But without faith it is impossible to please him: for he that cometh to God must believe that he is, and that he is a rewarder of them that diligently seek him. *Mirror Him*

Max

Max did not think of himself as being cool. He never thought of himself as uncool. In fact, Max did not think of himself much at all. Max just thought of himself as being part of our family and that was enough for him.

Oh wait, I am getting a little ahead of my story. Let me back up to the very beginning and start over.

When I was a youngster, I liked or disliked rather quickly without much thought as to why. Sometime later I would find out that I regretted some of my choices. As I got older, I took more time deciding whether I liked or disliked something.

You see, one of the things that I did not care for as a youth, was cats. I was never mean to any cat; I just did not care for them much. That was most likely due to our family only having dogs as I grew up. My sister Betsy wanted a cat when we were growing up but never had one.

After I enlisted in the US Navy, Betsy my middle sister, got her first cat. It was part Persian, part Siamese, and part who knows what. I had come home on leave to find a cat now residing at our house. One day I notice the cat acting very odd. Betsy's cat was lying under a hedge by the street curb. This was not unusual, but the cat seemed to be expecting something. It kept looking up the street and then down the street.

I called dad outside and asked, "what on earth is that cat was doing". He replied, "Oh that cat does that from time to time, just keep watching". So I waited and watch the cat.

About half an hour had passed before, a considerable size dog came strolling down the street. He was minding his own business and seemed to not have a care. He was not bothering anything or anyone. But the dog was walking close to the curb which would bring him very close to the cat.

The dog had just passed the cat when it suddenly happened. The cat sprang from under the hedges and pounced on the rear of the dog. It sunk its teeth into the top of the dog's rump. With all four paws, claws extended, it began raking both sides of the dog's flank. The dog let out a very painful yelp and took off. I watched as the dog disappeared over a slight hill two blocks away. The cat was still clinging to the back of the dog which was still yelping.

Five minutes later, the cat came strolling back into our yard. The cat now had a smile on its face and its chest poked out proudly. Dad informed me that this cat did that from time to time. That was the first cat that I liked. I know that was not right for me to like a cat for that reason. Yes, I am sorry about that now.

You know, Satan is a lot like that cat. We may be minding our own business when suddenly, Satan pounces on us. It pays to be a child of God at a time such as this. With God, we have help in the time of such an attack. We have the assurance that He will never leave us or forsake us.

Psalms 46:1 God is our refuge and strength, a very present help in trouble.

Now back to the present day. It was one of those rainy Florida days where it seemed to rain all day. There had been a heavy overcast and thunderstorms in the area. I love it when it rains. I love to listen to the sound of rain as it hits a tin roof. The sound that it makes as it trickles down the downspout. The air is cool and clean, and it gives a rebirth to nature. I even love to drive in the rain. Of course, one must slow down and drive with extra caution.

I had just driven thirty-seven miles from work and pulled into our yard. As I gathered my stuff from the seat, I checked to see just how hard the rain was dripping from our Oak-tree. I opened the driver's door and hurried to the front stoop.

As I stepped onto the front stoop, I saw something that was not there when I left that morning. There were two full-grown cats and three kittens smiling up at me. I thought, "Where in the world did you all come from?" Until this day, our family had not had a cat.

All five cats were looking up at me with a look on their faces that said, "Welcome Home." Instantly, my wife thought the cats were just fine being at our house. Thus, the cats were to stay and stay forever.

Over the next few days, we realized that the largest of the five cats was the mother, the father, and three kittens. The mother was a gentle white cat with large gray patches. We knew this was the mother because she was still nursing the three kittens.

The father cat was a large tiger stripe gray with a white chest, tummy, and paws. We assumed this was the father cat as he was always looking after the three kittens. If the kittens came too close to the edge of the stoop, he would gently nudge them closer to the house. It wasn't until days later that we found out that this male cat was from the previous litter.

It was almost two weeks before our daughter Stacy stopped by. She marveled over the cats and thought it was great that we had more pets. We only had one small dog prior to the arrival of the cats.

Stacy played with the cats for a few minutes and then asked what we were going to name them. We had not given names much thought at this point. She was so helpful in suggesting names for each one. The large white and gray mama cat she said looked like a Maria and the tiger-stripe gray looked like a Max. She did not suggest names for the kittens.

We told her that they were not staying and that we were going to find them a loving home. To this, she objected and gave reasons why we should keep them all.

We told her that we did not want litter after litter of kittens. To which she replied, "But Maria has been spayed." To which we asked, "How do you know?" "See the scar on her tummy," she said? To which we replied, "You have not looked at that cat's stomach. How do you know she has been spayed?"

It was not until then that we began putting the clues together. We realized that the cats belonged to our daughter Stacy. When we confronted her, she finally admitted that the kittens had been born at her house. Stacy continued with her confession. Maria was the mother to the three kittens but Max, the 'tiger-stripe gray' was Maria's son. So Max was from Maria's first litter and the in-between brother of the three kittens.

As the confession continued, the truth really began to emerge. Stacy and our two granddaughters Brittany and Lindsey had decided to find the cats a loving home. So, they loaded all five cats in the car and drove to our house. They pulled up to our driveway, unloaded the cats, and shooed them towards our house. When the cats went to our front door, Stacy and the girls drove off.

By this time, my wife was enjoying the cute kittens playing and decided to keep them all. Over time, the three kittens found good homes, but Maria and Max remained. Maria and Max were a part of our family now. They both worked their way into our hearts, and we enjoyed both of them very much.

Maria was the gentle loving type. She was quiet and did not get into any kind of trouble. She remained close to home and was always ready for a little attention. Not to mention that she followed me around like a little dog. To this day I cannot venture into our front yard without her getting close to me. I must always look down before I move my feet.

Max, on the other hand, was a fellow who loved adventure. He would slowly begin walking out of the yard and down the street. When you ask him, "Max, where are you going," he would stop, look back at you, meow, and then keep going.

Max was a talker. Upon his return home, he would always check in with multiple meows. You could ask him where he had gone, and he would tell you as best as he could. You could always enjoy a complete conversation with Max. Just ask him questions and he would keep answering you for half an hour or more.

After his return home or on a sunny day, you could find Max lying in one of the outside chairs. There under the shade of the oak tree, he would spend many relaxing hours. He would lay there, upside down with all four feet in the air. His head was also upside down, perhaps as a way to keep his mouth closed as he slept. Perhaps, the world just looked a little better upside down to him. Either way, he was at peace with the world in the chair, in the shade of that old oak tree.

Max never started a fight with other cats, but he never backed down either. That was the reason for his floppy ears. Perhaps, his ears were a result of his courting the lady cats of the neighborhood. Either way, we felt sorry for his little scared and floppy ears.

A few months ago, we noticed that Max had lost a good deal of his weight. In fact, he was no longer a fat healthy cat but skin and bones. He lost all that weight in a matter of a couple of weeks.

We quickly realized that he would not eat much of the dry cat food. Our neighbor had suggested that we soften his food. So, for the month or more, we had been feeding him canned cat food. Sometimes I would mix dry cat food with a little water to soften it. He loved that combination and for a time, added a little weight. We began feeding him four or five times a day. But he just did not gain the weight back.

Max was born an outside cat as was his mother. In the twelve-plus years that he was part of our family, he never tried to come into the house. Then after he lost the weight, he would follow one of us inside every chance he got.

Once inside, he always did the same thing. He would walk down the hall looking at each door. Then he would return to the living room and just sit down. One day I walked into our living room and there was Max. He was just lying on my footstool; content as could be. Neither my wife nor I, knew when he had sneaked in. He remained on the footstool until he was ready to go back out.

It was just yesterday, that I mentioned to my wife that I had not seen Max that day. I told her that it was not like him not to be around. For the past few weeks, every time anyone opened the front door, Max would spring to his feet and come running. If we did not have his food container in hand, he would meow several times. But today, Max was not there by the door. He was not by the door all day long.

It was not until late afternoon that my wife called my name with urgency. I could tell by her tone that something was wrong. As we met by the corner of our house she stated, "I think that Max died. Sure enough, as I look around the corner of the house, there was Max. He was lying in one of our flower beds on a soft bed of Hibiscus leaves. The last place that Max laid down was on the outside of a wall at our house. On the other side of that wall in the same area, was where I lay my head at night to sleep. Was that a coincidence or was he trying to get as close to us as he could? We will never know the answer to that.

Mine and my wife's hearts just broke upon finding that Max had died. He had become such an integral part of our family for twelve plus years. He had such an easy-going disposition. He was the only male cat that I ever knew that liked his chest and tummy rubbed. Max, you will remain in our hearts forever and will be greatly missed.

When a family member, friend, or beloved pet passes from this life, it reminds us of our own mortality. It reminds us that we will not be upon this earth forever. There is a point in time when our time here will be over. Are you ready for that? If you have not become one of God's children, you are not ready. If you do not know Jesus Christ as your personal Lord and Savior, you will not be ready.

Romans 10:9 If you declare with your mouth, "Jesus is Lord," and believe in your heart that God raised him from the dead, you will be saved.

How does someone get ready for passing from this life into the next? It is simple and easy to prepare for. Simply say, "Heavenly Father, I believe that Jesus Christ, is your only begotten son. I believe that Jesus Christ, died on the cross to save me from my sins. I believe that You, raised Him from the grave on the third day and He is now interceding for me. Lord Jesus, come into my heart and save me. Be my Lord and Savior. Amen.

If you said that simple prayer and believe it in your heart, you are saved. But it does not stop there. You owe it to yourself to read His Holy Word. He will lead you to understand. Select a Bible that is true to the last dot. Look at the verse **John 3:16**. If the word **begotten** is not in that verse, find another Bible. Read your Bible every day. Find a good church where you can fellowship with other believers in Christ Jesus.

Hebrews 10:25 Not forsaking the assembling of ourselves together, as the manner of some is but exhorting one another: and so much the more, as you see the Day approaching

Please do not wait, as your time may be sooner than you think. No one can pray you through to heaven after you are gone. No one can make the decision for you. You must decide for yourself where you will be for all of eternity. My prayer for you is God's love and blessings and not curses that you may have brought upon yourself. Remember, when you hear of someone dying, God is reminding you that one day it will be your turn. Please, be ready!

"What happened to Maria," you ask? She is still the queen of our front yard. She remains pleasingly plump, happy, and loved.

Mirror Him

The Dream

Last night, I had a dream. It was not an ordinary dream but one that caused me to stop in my tracks and think. As I do anytime that I have a dream that is unpleasant, I rebuked it in the name of Jesus Christ. The word rebuke means: To reprimand; strongly warn or **restrain**. I not only rebuked this dream but bound it in the name of Jesus and cast it out (sent away). According to the Bible, we have the power through Jesus to bind things here on earth. The Bible tells us that whatever we bind on earth, will also be bound in Heaven.

Mathew 16:19 And I will give unto you the keys of the kingdom of heaven: and whatsoever you shalt bind on earth shall be bound in heaven: and whatsoever you shalt loose on earth shall be loosed in heaven.

So, what was this dream about that was so unsettling? I dreamed that I was in the hallway of my home. It was very dark, so it must have been late at night or early in the morning. There stood before me a large, figure of a person.

I understood that he was going to take me to a place that I could not come back from.

I did not have a choice but had to go with him. There seemed to be a doorway to our left during this dream that we were about to step through. But I remembered, there is no door in that location.

My wife was sound asleep, and I was not allowed to wake her to tell her goodbye. I asked if I could take a change of clothes with me. I was told no, that I would not need them.

At that moment, our little dog Sophie jumped up on my leg. I picked her up and held her close. I rubbed her as I always do. I explained to her that she could not go with me. I also told her that she needed to stay here and take care of mama (my wife) and Sissy (our other small dog). I told her that I had to go but would wait for them. She licked my hand as I petted her before easing her back down on the floor. I softly told her to go back to bed and she turned and headed off.

It was at this moment that I woke up and began rebuking the dream. I also began thinking about the previous years of my life. Had I lived my life as best as I could? Could I have made decisions better in my past? Could I have made choices more in line with the Bible's teaching? Could my choices have been more in line with the word of God? The answer was a resounding, yes. I believe that almost every person would answer yes to that question if they were honest with themselves. But Jesus! Jesus took our place on the cross to pay our sin debt. That is if we will accept Him as our Lord and Savior.

It was then that I became flooded with thoughts of my family. Our children live a decent life, but is it good enough to secure an eternal, heavenly home? They believe in God but do not go to church as they should. I worry that they have not taught their children the things of God as they should have. I worry about what kind of example they have set for their children. No, I am not judging anyone. I am merely looking at what I see in their lives and remembering what the Bible says. That in and of itself is not judging but comparing. I am looking at their lives as I am my own. I believe that is called evaluating.

All sorts of things run through one's mind after such a dream as this. How will my spouse get by without me? Will our children step up and fill the gap that my leaving will surely cause? I pray that they will, but I somehow doubt that they can adequately fill my shoes the way I did. Is that a little presumptuous of me? At the present time and the way that my family seems, I do not think so.

Isaiah 25:8 He will swallow up death in victory, and the Lord GOD will wipe away tears from off all faces; and the rebuke of his people shall he take away from off all the earth: for the LORD hath spoken it.

Revelation 17:7 He will swallow up death in victory, and the Lord GOD will wipe away tears from off all faces; and the rebuke of his people shall he take away from off all the earth: for the LORD hath spoken it.

Revelation 21:4 And God shall wipe away all tears from their eyes; and there shall be no more death, neither sorrow, nor crying, neither shall there be any more pain: for the former things are passed away.

2 Corinthians 5:6 Therefore we are always confident, knowing that, whilst we are at home in the body, we are absent from the Lord:

At first, I was incredibly sad about my leaving. It was then that I remembered the above scriptures. It is my belief that when we die, we step quickly into our eternal life. I believe this because that is what the Bible says about death. In one instant we are here, the next blink of an eye, we are there. Once we are there, we are instantly in the presence of our Lord. If we have lived according to God's word, we will be instantly surrounded and filled with love and peace. It will be love and peace greater than we have ever known. We will be filled with the love that we have been searching for our entire lives. At that moment, our joy will be so overwhelming that all our cares will vanish.

Before I retired, we had a saying at work. The saying was, "everyone's name is written in pencil so they can erase it anytime they want to."

As humans, we think it will not happen to us, at least not for quite some time. We think we have time left before we must leave this world. But none of us knows when our time will be up. It could happen today, tonight, or sometime in the future.

My Uncle Bill and Aunt Shirley had been working in their yard when a neighbor stopped by. Uncle Bill knelt beside the neighbor's car and talked to the neighbor for several minutes. The man and Uncle Bill said their goodbyes as Uncle Bill stood up. Uncle Bill turned to walk away, he took two steps toward Aunt Shirley and fell dead. Uncle Bill had a heart attack without any warning.

It can happen without any advance notice, and it doesn't have to be health related. I myself had an extremely close call with lightning one afternoon. Back then, I drove a Datsun pickup truck. The old truck needed sparkplug wires badly. At times I would drive through a water puddle and splashing water would drown the engine. For that reason, I carried a can of WD-40 in my truck. When the engine drowned out, I would spray the sparkplug wires with the WD-40 and the engine would run again.

I was on my way home during a sudden Florida thunderstorm. As I drove through a water puddle, the engine drowned out and stopped running. I let the truck coast onto the grass in the middle of the four-lane highway. I grabbed the WD-40, got out in the pouring rain, and sprayed the sparkplug wires. I was then able to start my truck but noticed another Datsun truck must have had the same issue. The other truck was sitting in the fast lane of a four-lane highway and not moving. It had stopped about two blocks in front of where I had stopped.

I drove onto the grass in the middle of the road and beside the other truck. I shouted to the other driver, "Is it drowned out?" He replied, "Yes". I said, "Pop your hood open". I left the comfort of my truck; I hurried and raised the hood of his truck. The other driver quickly joined me and was holding his truck hood open for me to spray his sparkplug wires.

The other driver's truck had stalled part way up a hill. By this time, water flowing down the hill in the roadway was ankle-deep.

I began to spray his sparkplug wires with the WD-40 when suddenly, every hair on my body stood on end. This was followed within seconds by a blinding flash of white light followed by a deafening boom. I could see absolutely nothing but white for what seemed like a few seconds. As I was blinded by the flash of white light, I was also hit in my head very forcefully. I thought I had been hit by lightning for sure.

As my vision returned, I could see the cloth welders cap that I had been wearing land in the water below the truck's engine. It soon disappeared as it flowed with the water under the truck. I quickly stood up, still thinking about being struck by lightning, and ran around the truck. I was able to catch my welder's cap as it flowed with the water from underneath the back of the truck.

As my hand caught my welder's cap, I realized something. I realized that I had not been hit by lightning although it came way too close for comfort. I came to the realization that the driver that I had just helped had dropped his truck's hood on my head. He had been holding the hood open to help me but was startled by the extremely close lightning strike.

It was then that I heard his truck start and very quickly start driving away. This left me completely soaked to the bone by the rain, standing in the middle of the fast lane of Hwy 301 holding my can of WD-40, looking, and feeling very foolish. I couldn't help but wonder what the other drivers thought as they drove by.

The point here is not to stop helping people or that people are ungrateful, but rather to be ready. We do not know when our time on Earth will be over, so be ready. Live your life for God and be ready whenever your time to leave here has come.

James 4:14 Whereas ye know not what shall be on the morrow. For what is your life? It is even a vapor, that appeared for a little time, and then vanishes away.

Am I ready to leave planet Earth? No, I am not. I still have things I need to take care of. I still have things that I would like to do for the kingdom of God. But life is like the game Hide and Seek. Everyone gets ready as one person covers their eyes and begins counting to ten. As the count begins, everyone runs and hides. Once the person counting reaches the number ten, they announce in a loud voice, "ready or not, here I come." Then the person who counted to ten tries to find and tag the children who hid. In the same way, ready or not, our life could be over. We will not have time to say goodbye. No time to take care of that last-minute thing. There will be no time to ask God for forgiveness. I ask myself and you, are we ready?

If your answer to the previous question is, "I'm not sure." Please join me in truly and honestly evaluating our lives. I believe that you will come to the same conclusion that I have. My conclusion is that there is more room in my life for God than I now give Him. So, I have made the decision that I will seek Him more each day. I will read His Holy Word more often than I do now. I will find good things for my mind to think about. I will turn away from the things that cause strife in my life. I will stay away from the things that God does not approve of. I will try to live my life as a better example so others can see God in me. I will look for things for my hands to do to further His kingdom. For we, by the grace of God, will live with Him in His kingdom forever.

So, the question now is, how do I obtain the grace of God? First, we must believe in our hearts that God is. We must believe in our hearts that Jesus is the Only Begotten Son of God. We must believe in our hearts that Jesus died for our sins and rose again on the third day. We must believe in our hearts that Jesus now sits by the right side of our Heavenly Father interceding for you and me. We must pray and ask Jesus Christ to be our Lord and Savior. We must ask God and Jesus to forgive us of all our sins and cover them in the precious blood of Jesus. We must live the remainder of our lives according to the word of God as best we can. Ask God for the strength, determination, and wisdom to do His will. He will help you in these areas but will not do it for you. It will take effort on our part to reach heaven.

Do Not let yourself wander away from Him. Where we spend eternity depends upon our choices. I do not believe we will be able to blame any of our choices on someone else. If we allow someone to influence our choices in a negative way, we are allowing them to control our lives. We must allow God to guide us in everything that we think, do, and speak.

Mirror Him

Borrowed Time

Ecclesiastes 3:1 To everything there is a season and a time to every purpose under the heaven:

Ecclesiastes 3:2 A time to be born, and a time to die; a time to plant, and a time to pluck up that which is *planted.*

Ecclesiastes 3:3 A time to kill, and a time to heal; a time to break down, and a time to build up.

Ecclesiastes 3:4 A time to weep, and a time to laugh; a time to mourn, and a time to dance.

Ecclesiastes 3:5 A time to cast away stones, and a time to gather stones together; a time to embrace, and a time to refrain from embracing.

Ecclesiastes 3:6 A time to get, and a time to lose; a time to keep, and a time to cast away.

Ecclesiastes 3:7 A time to tear, and a time to sew; a time to keep silence, and a time to speak.

Ecclesiastes 3:8 A time to love, and a time to hate; a time of war, and a time of peace.

The Bible says, there is a time for everything under the sun. God has planned everything from the beginning to the end and back again. He is the only one in full control. He is in full control of absolutely everything except you and me. You see, God gave each of us a "Free Will". That means, we get to decide or choose certain things for ourselves.

With "Free Will", we have no one to blame but ourselves. When we choose or decide correctly, we receive rewards. When we choose or decide incorrectly, there are consequences. With that said, please remember that all good things come from God. All negative things come when God steps aside because of an incorrect choice that we have made. That allows Satan to step in with consequences and terrible things. So, it is we ourselves that cause our problems, the margarita of the time. It is only when we stay in the will of God, that we have help and hope through Him.

Luke 12:4 And I say unto you my friends, be not afraid of them that kill the body, and after that have no more that they can do.

Luke 12:5 But I will forewarn you whom you shall fear: Fear Him, which after he

hath killed hath power to cast into hell; yes, I say unto you, Fear Him.

Luke 12:6 Are not five sparrows sold for two farthings (a farthing is worth about ¼ of a penny)***, and not one of them is forgotten before God?***

Luke 12:7 But even the very hairs of your head are all numbered. Fear not, therefore: you are of more value than many sparrows.

If God knows and has planned everything from beginning to end, does He ever change His mind? The answer is, "Yes" God does change His mind from time to time.

The Bible tells us, that God sent Isaiah to Hezekiah to tell him to get his house in order because he was going to die. Hezekiah prayed to God, reminding Him that he was a godly man. Hezekiah reminded God that he had kept all His commandments, all of his life. God sent Isaiah back to Hezekiah to tell him that He had added fifteen years to his life.

Isaiah 38:5 Go, and say to Hezekiah, thus says the LORD, the God of David thy father, I have heard thy prayer, I have seen your tears: behold, I will add unto thy days fifteen years.

Isaiah 46:9 Remember the former things of old: for I am God, and there is none else; I am God, and there is none like me,

Isaiah 46:10 Declaring the end from the beginning, and from ancient times the things that are not yet done, saying, my counsel shall stand, and I will do all my pleasure:

God is so awesome to reward us when we follow Him and believe in Jesus. We simply need to remember to be patient and have faith in Him. God will work all things out for good to those who love Him.

Yes, God can change the plans of men as well. God can also speed up or slow down time itself.

Matthew 24:22 And except those days should be shortened, there should no flesh be saved: but for the elect's sake, those days shall be shortened.

Genesis 5:5 And all the days that Adam lived were nine hundred and thirty years: and he died.

Genesis 5:6 And Seth lived a hundred and five years, and begat Enos:

Genesis 5:7 And Seth lived after he begat Enos eight hundred and seven years, and begat sons and daughters:

Genesis 5:8 And all the days of Seth were nine hundred and twelve years: and he died.

Genesis 5:9 And Enos lived ninety years, and begat Cain:

Genesis 5:10 And Enos lived after he begat Cain eight hundred and fifteen years, and begat sons and daughters:

Genesis 5:11 And all the days of Enos were nine hundred and five years: and he died.

Genesis 5:12 And Cain lived seventy years, and begat Mahalalel:

Genesis 5:13 And Cain lived after he begat Mahalalel eight hundred and forty years, and begat sons and daughters:

Genesis 5:14 And all the days of Cain were nine hundred and ten years: and he died.

Genesis 5:15 And Mahalalel lived sixty and five years, and begat Jared:

Genesis 5:16 And Mahalalel lived after he begat Jared eight hundred and thirty years, and begat sons and daughters:

Genesis 5:17 And all the days of Mahalalel were eight hundred ninety and five years: and he died.

In the beginning of the Bible, those who worshiped God, lived much longer than we do today. The longer a person lives, the longer the world can corrupt their thinking and their soul. Just think how corrupt the world would be if everyone lived that long today. That is unless everyone lived by God's commandments.

For that reason, God has shortened the life span of man. God will return soon to gather His children. How do we know the return of God's only begotten son Jesus is soon to happen? Answer: by watching for the signs listed in our Bible. The disciples asked Jesus what the signs would be of His soon return. In **Matthew 24:3 through Matthew 24:14**, Jesus gave the answer.

Jesus gave a list of things that would happen prior to His return. The list is as follows: Take heed that no man deceives you for many will come in His name saying, I am Christ. You will hear of wars and rumors of wars. There will be famines, pestilences, and earthquakes in many places. You will be disliked because you love God and are a Christian. People will be offended and will betray one another. There will be false prophets and they will deceive people. There are people who will not know what love is. But Jesus said, "He that endures unto the end shall be saved". Jesus also said that when this gospel of the kingdom is preached all over the world, then shall the end come.

When you look outside and see the dark clouds gathering you think, today it is going to rain. When you step outside in the morning and you feel a slight chill in the air you think, winter will soon be here. When we watch the news and know what the Bible tells us, we know that Jesus' return is much closer than we think. In fact, you can feel it as you do the chill of a fall morning. The question is, are you ready to meet Jesus, face to face? Are we ready to stand before God Himself and give an account for our lives?

Some of you have read of where my faith roots first sprouted. For the rest of you, my faith root sprouted in The Ruskin Tabernacle in Ruskin, Florida. It was there watching and listening to the teachings and preaching of Pastor Rosa Sikes that my spirit man was reborn. Seeing many of God's miracles occur within my own family, I knew that I was in the right place. I also knew beyond any doubt that what I was being taught and what I was reading in my Bible was the absolute truth.

Sometimes I may not know why things happen as they do but I retain my faith that God is working things out for my good. I have come to realize over the years that when I do not understand something in the Bible, it is due to a lack of my own knowledge and understanding. This however never causes my faith to waver. I have seen many miracles from God and have seen the proof.

John 20:29 Jesus said unto him, Thomas because you have seen me, you believed: blessed are they that have not seen, and yet have believed.

There was during my upbringing in this church, that something very odd happened. There were older people within the congregation who were on Social Security. When they received their checks for one month, printed on them was a message. The printed message said, **"Do Not Cash Unless the Number 666 Appears"**.

Each letter of the Israeli alphabet has a numeric value. Whoever the beast of Revelations in the Bible is, the letters of his name will equal 666.

Revelation 13:16 And he caused all, both small and great, rich, and poor, free and bond (slave), ***to receive a mark in their right hand, or in their foreheads:***

Revelation 13:17 And that no man might buy or sell unless he has the mark, or the name of the beast, or the number of his name.

Revelations 13:18 Here is wisdom. Let him that hath understanding count the number of the beast: for it is the number of a man; and his number is Six hundred threescore and

Why is this significant? If a person has not received the "mark of the beast", they will not be able to buy or sell anything. How does one get the mark of the beast? By swearing an oath of allegiance to and worshiping the beast.

By accepting his mark on either the forehead or the palm of their right hand, a person will be able to buy or sell. When a person has done this, they lose their soul forever. There is no forgiveness for taking the mark of the beast. At this point, one has denounced the one true God.

Who is the beast? The beast is a demonic entity that will rule the earth for seven years. This will be the New World Order. The beast will eventually set himself up as God.

These older people carried their Social Security checks to Sister Sikes to show her the message printed on them. Sister Sikes prayed with them. Then she instructed them to call the Social Security Office. When they called the people at the Social Security Office, they were very apologetic. They said, "**We are so sorry. Those checks were not supposed to be printed until 1967**".

Yes, you read that correctly and I did not mistype the year. Are you shocked? Are you alarmed? We should all be alarmed if we are not a child of God. We should be very alarmed if we have not accepted Jesus Christ as our Lord and Savior. He alone is the only way to escape these things that are sure to come.

John 14:6 Jesus said unto him, I am the way, the truth, and the life: no man comes unto the Father but by me.

As of 1967, we have been living on borrowed time. God in His infinite wisdom has delayed Jesus' return to allow all that will to accept Him as their Lord and Savior. If you have not done so already, WHAT ARE YOU WAITING FOR? Do not put it off any longer. Be sure of where you stand with God. Jesus

Christ will return, in a twinkle of an eye and there will not be time to pray. If you are not ready, get ready now.

Those of us who have accepted Jesus Christ as our Lord and Savior have eternal life and hope given to us by God. Children of God are not alarmed because God has prepared an escape for us. We are however genuinely concerned for those who have not accepted Jesus Christ as their Lord and Savior. Those born into the spirit of God will be caught up before the great wrath that will take place on earth. This catching up, we refer to it and call it The Rapture. However; the word Rapture does not appear in the Bible.

1 Thessalonians 4:17 For the Lord Himself shall descend from heaven with a shout, with the voice of the archangel, and with the trump of God: and the dead in Christ shall rise first:

1 Thessalonians 4:17 Then we which are alive and remain shall be caught up together with them in the clouds, to meet the Lord in the air: and so, shall we ever be with the Lord.

Luke 21:36 Watch you, therefore, and pray always, that you may be accounted worthy to escape all these things that shall come to pass and to stand before the Son of man.

Romans 2:3 And think you this, O man, that judge them which do such things, and do the same, that you shalt escape the judgment of God?

Are you a child of God? Have you been born into the family of God? If not, would you like to be? God has made it so easy for you to become one of His children. First, we must believe in our hearts that God is, and that Jesus Christ is the son of God who died to save us from sin.

But you may say, "I was not raised in a Christian home and have not lived a Christian life according to the Bible". Well, I am here to let you know that God loves you and that nothing else matters at this point.

Act 10:34 Then Peter opened his mouth, and said, of a truth, I perceive that God is no respecter of persons:

Act 2:21 And it shall come to pass, that whosoever shall call on the name of the Lord shall be saved.

John 3:16 For God so loved the world, that he gave his only begotten Son, that whosoever believeth in him should not perish, but have everlasting life.

John 3:17 For God sent not his Son into the world to condemn the world; but that the world through him might be saved.

John 3:18 He that believeth on him is not condemned: but he that believeth not is condemned already because he hath not believed in the name of the only begotten Son of God.

John 3:16 above says, "whosoever". Are you a "whosoever"? I am! A "whosoever" means anyone. Anyone who believes in their heart that God sent His only **begotten** son into this world to save all who would accept Him as Savior, you can be saved. If you are not saved already, please do not miss this opportunity as it may be your last.

We must confess to Him that we are a sinner and ask Him to forgive and save us. We could say something like this; Heavenly Father, I have sinned, and I know that I need you. Heavenly Father, I know that Jesus is your only begotten son. I know that Jesus Christ died to save me from sin. I know that Jesus Christ rose from the dead and now sits by your right hand. Dear Jesus Christ, please forgive me and save me. I will study your Holy word, live by your commandments, and worship you for the rest of my life. Amen!

If you said that prayer and really meant it with all your heart, you are now a child of God. You will also feel God's presents after saying that prayer. Now you must pursue and seek God with all your strength. You must read your Bible daily and ask the Holy Spirit to help you understand it. You should attend a church where you can worship and serve God.

Why should we attend a good church? So, we can learn more about God and Heaven. We must read our Bible along with the person reading theirs to ensure truth and accuracy. We should attend a good church, so we have support from other Christians. We need to uplift and encourage each other. We should help others by praying for them continually.

How do we know if it is a good church that we are in? That is a great question. I define a good church as one that the Holy Spirit leads me to. It is one where the Bible is directly preached from and not solely from a pastor's notes. It is a church where the pastor tells us what we need to correct in our lives to ensure a happy eternity. This is important because our soul will never die, and we want to be in a good place after this life.

Psalms 111:1 Praise the LORD! I will thank the LORD with all my heart as I meet with His godly people.

May God richly bless and guide you as you seek Him. May His love and mercy surround you as you climb ever higher in His love and wisdom. May you always be filled with joy and be a blessing to others as you share the knowledge of God. May you always follow Jesus with fervor. May you read God's Holy Word daily and remain in His blessings always. Amen

1Timothy 4:10 For therefore we both labor and suffer reproach, because we trust in the living God, who is the Savior of all men, especially of those that believe.

1Timothy 4:11 These things command and teach.

1Timothy 4:12 Let no man despise your youth; but be an example of the believers, in word, in conversation, in charity, in spirit, in faith, in purity.

1Timothy 4:13 Till I come, give attendance to reading, to exhortation, to doctrine. *(Read your Bible)*

1Timothy 4:14 Do not neglect the gift that is in you, which was given you by prophecy, with the laying on of the hands of the presbytery (church elders)*.*

1Timothy 4:15 Meditate upon these things; give yourself wholly to them; so that your profiting may appear to all.

1Timothy 4:16 Take heed unto yourself, and unto the doctrine; continue in them: for in doing this you will both save yourself, and them that hear you.

Philippians 4:6 Be careful for nothing, but in everything by prayer and supplication with thanksgiving let your requests be made known unto God.

Philippians 4:7 And the peace of God, which passes all understanding, shall keep your hearts and minds through Christ Jesus.

Philippians 4:8 Finally, brethren, whatsoever things are true, whatsoever things are honest, whatsoever things are just, whatsoever things are pure, whatsoever things are lovely, whatsoever things are of good report; if there be any virtue, and if there be any praise, think on these things.

Philippians 4:9 Those things, which you have both learned, and received, and heard, and seen in me, do: and the God of peace shall be with you.

Mirror Him

David and Goliath

In the Bible, 1st Samuel, the sixteenth chapter, begins telling the story of a shepherd boy who watched over sheep. His job was to watch over, care for and protect the sheep. It would seem like such a menial job, but God had great plans for David.

While watching the flock of sheep, David had killed a lion and a bear using only a sling, sort of a modern-day slingshot. Apparently, David was very good with a sling.

One day, his king's army was fighting a battle with another kingdom. It was often the custom in those days, for each army to pick a champion. A man that each army thought could fight and win. These two armies would let their champions fight, and whichever man won, his army would be the victor. It was a simple way to determine which army won without a lot of men being killed.

The Israelites had not picked a champion. But the Philistine army had chosen Goliath. Goliath was a huge giant, and everyone was terrified of him. Goliath would come out and yell awful things to the Israelites. He even cursed the God of the Israelites and taunted them.

David had arrived at the camp of the Israelites with food for his brothers. He saw Goliath and saw what he was doing. David heard the awful thing that Goliath was saying. David wanted to know what the Israelites were going to do about Goliath. But no one was willing to go out and face Goliath in combat.

It was then that David, the shepherd boy, volunteered to fight Goliath. They suited David with King Soul's armor and his sword. But the armor and sword were way too heavy for David. Instead of armor and sword, David took the sling that he had always used to protect the sheep.

On his way to fight Goliath, David had to cross a stream. He paused for a few moments at the stream. He picked up five smooth stones and placed them in his pouch. Why did David pick up five stones for one giant? Because Goliath had brothers!

When Goliath saw the boy, he shouted at David, "Come closer, little one. I will kill you and give your flesh to the birds of the air, and your bones to the wild beasts.".

Goliath knew that he had an advantage when it came to fighting up close. Listen closely and you can almost hear the distasteful, condescending tone in Goliath's booming voice. Can't you hear it?

David placed one stone in his sling and said, "You come against me with spear and sword. But I come against you in the name of God Almighty." With that said, David ran toward Goliath swinging his sling around. David swung the sling around and released the smooth stone. The stone struck Goliath in the center of his forehead and sunk deep into his head. Goliath fell to the ground with a loud thud. The smooth stone had found its mark and Goliath was dead. David ran to Goliath, took Goliath's sword, and cut off Goliath's head. The Israelites won the battle with God's help and a simple sling.

Is there a Goliath in your life? Do you hear the booming voice of a Goliath in your life saying, "Come closer, little one"? I do not mean an actual giant. I am speaking of a spiritual giant. I mean something that is too big for you to manage by yourself. Is there a mountain too high for you to climb? Is there a river too wide for you to cross? Do you have a situation in your life that you just don't know how to handle? Is there a problem or temptations in your life that are too complicated and large for you to solve? Is there a burden of grief that you can no longer bear by yourself?

Well, I know a man who can help you. His name is Jesus Christ. Yes, He is a way maker and a problem solver. Have you called upon Him? Take your problem to Jesus Christ. He specializes in things that are impossible for us. There is nothing too small or too large for Him to fix. He is a friend, provider, healer, counselor, intercessor between you and God, comforter, Savior, and much more.

Take all your cares to Him in prayer and lay them at His feet. Once you have given your problems and cares to God, don't worry about them any longer. You could not solve your problem with worry before. Why continue to worry about them now. Your problems are in good hands if you have truly given them to God. If you continue to worry about your problems, it is as though you are telling God that you don't believe He can handle them.

As with anything else, we must be proactive. We must think ahead of what our actions could cause. We must do everything that we possibly can to keep problems from popping up in our lives. Yes, we must try to solve problems that arise ourselves. But when we have done all that we can, it is time to take that problem to God in prayer.

God specializes in things that seem impossible. When the doctors have given up,

God can heal it. When we have a broken heart, He is the only one who can mend it. When we have an empty place in our hearts, He can fill it. If grief filles you, He can ease the pain. When you are at your darkest point, Jesus is the light of the world. When you think that you don't have a friend, Jesus is always there for you. He will listen to you when no one else will. Give Jesus Christ a chance and you will see for yourself.

How do you give Jesus Christ a chance, you ask? By believing in your heart that Jesus Christ is the only begotten son of God. That He was crucified so that your sins will be forgiven. Believing that he rose from the grave on the third day and now sits by God's right hand. Yes, He is sitting there interceding for you and me.

If you believe that deep in your heart, then repeat after me. Heavenly Father, God of Abraham, Isaac, and Jacob, I know that I have sinned. I am lost and in need of a Savior. Please come into my life. Wash me and make me whole. I will read and live by God's Holy word, worship, and serve you. Please be my Lord and Savior. In Jesus' Holy name I pray, Amen.

If you said that simple prayer, you are now a child of God. Live by the promises that you just made to God and God will keep His promises to you. What are God's promises, you ask? Read the Bible and you will find out all about the wonderful promises of God. That is only one of the reasons you should read the Bible daily. Each day that you read your Bible, God will reveal Himself, and more of His truth and promises to you.

David went on to become greatly blessed after he slew Goliath. But you do not have to kill a giant to be blessed. To be blessed, all one must do is accept Jesus Christ as their Lord and Savior, have faith in God, read the Holy Bible daily, and live their life accordingly. May God bless and keep you is my prayer for you. Amen!

Mirror Him

Early Hour Dream

I stated early on in this book that many of my dreams had actually come to pass. This may be one that I pray does not come to pass. But God's will be done. The point here is to always be obedient to God.

In the pre-dawn hours of this morning, I had a dream. You may say, "so what, I have dreams all of the time." Remember early in this book, I said to write your dreams down and tell your family? That will verify your dream later as either something that your mind made up while entertaining itself or a message from Heaven.

No matter what your dream is or how strange, write it down. In the Bible is an account of Joseph and a dream pharaoh had. The account begins in Genesis 41:1 and goes through verse 57. You can read it for yourself later, but for now, I will tell you.

Pharaoh had a dream where seven fat cows came up out of a river. After them, came up out of the river seven skinny cows who ate the first seven. Then the pharaoh dreamed of a stalk of grain and seven plump heads of grain sprang up on it. Then sprang up seven heads of grain that were weak and thin. Then the weak and thin heads of grain ate the seven plump heads. Then the pharaoh awoke. I think a dream that bizarre would have caused me to awake as well.

The pharaoh turned to David for the interpretation of the dream, who was in his dungeon. David told the pharaoh that God was showing him that there was going to be seven years of plenty. There would also be seven years of famine following the plenty. The pharaoh promoted David to ruler over all things, second only to pharaoh. David answered to no man but the pharaoh.

I relate this Bible story about David to illustrate, that every dream is worthy of writing down. You may not know what a dream means until sometime in the future, no matter how strange it may seem now. If the dream came from God, He will reveal its meaning in His time.

Now, back to my dream. Ok, so I am writing it down and right now you are the closest thing I have to the family that is awake.

I do not know where I was during this dream, but there were people all around me. A few of the people seemed to be in some sort of official capacity as they were checking papers that the horde of the people had. All of the people were showing their papers to these few that seemed to be in charge.

There was a man's voice, almost frantic by my side who was prodding me to do my best. In this dream, I was using a computer photo editing program to edit the papers for all these people. They would then show them to these officials.

Each time that I tried to edit the border of these documents, it came out different than what I had intended. The insistent voice by my side was saying to me, "You did it for all of those other people, you can do it again now." So, I tried again to get the border of the document updated and corrected.

I had it right but when I tried to update the document, it looked wrong. It wasn't until I became almost exasperated that I noticed teardrops had welled up in the corner of my eyes. The teardrops were altering what I was seeing. I could not make out what I had placed on the papers of these people. Satan was altering my vision.

It was at this point that I noticed teardrops welling up in the eyes of the officials. No wonder they were seeing the papers of these people as though they were perfect and letting them pass. God was altering the vision of the officials. What Satan meant for evil, God turned around and used it for good.

By now, I had realized that this horde of people, were God's children. But where had they come from? Where were they going? I do not have a clue! All I know is I was placed there to help them. During that short period of time, God was causing the officials to see what He wanted them to see.

It was then in my dream that I heard a very masculine, male voice. It said, "tell my people not to worry, I will see them through. That I will meet them at their problem." I knew exactly what that meant. But how can God meet you at your problem? By getting on your knees and seeking God in prayer. That is where God will meet you at your problem. Take everything to God in prayer. Seek Him out and benefit from His wisdom and His love for you. I am assuming that you are a Christian. If you are not a Christian, what are you waiting for? God deeply loves you and wants a personal relationship with you.

Here I would like to draw your attention to a song I heard many years ago. Some call it "Last Night as I Lay Sleeping". Others call it "Sorry I Never Knew You". Either way, search for either on YOUTUBE.COM. I feel it appropriate to mention this song here because it also is about a dream. It was written in late 1949 or early 1950. It is a wonderful song that will be sure to give everyone something to think about. Go on, do it for me and you too.

My question is if someone accused you or me of being a Christian, would there be enough evidence to convict us? Do our lives and character mirror Him? Are you one of God's children?

I realize that I have given you an invitation a couple of times to accept Jesus Christ as your Lord and Savior. But this decision is just too important to only mention it once. The decision to follow Him will be the most important and best decision that you will ever make.

If you have not received Jesus Christ as your Lord and Savior, now is the time. Please do not wait another moment. You have a blessed future to gain or a soul to lose. The choice is yours and yours alone.

Hopefully, you have chosen Jesus Christ. Good! Then you can repeat along with me. Dear Jesus Christ, son of the living God, I need you. Please forgive me for the sin, transgressions, iniquities in my life, and all that I have caused you to be displeased with me for. I believe you died for me and that you now sit by our Heavenly Father's right hand interceding for me. From this moment forward, I will worship and live my life for you. Be my Lord and Savior. Amen!

Now that you are a child of God, act like it. Study your Bible, attend a good Church, control your speech and vocabulary, and share Him with others. Be listening for God to speak to you and when He does, be obedient to His will.

Please remember that in the end, God's children win. We win a wonderful and eternal home, and we will be with our God forever and ever.

Be Greatly Blessed, share God's love, God's word, and Keep the Faith.

Mirror Him

Other Books by Larry E. O'Neal,

- Where Love and Grace Abides,
  My proof Positive

- Guide My Steps Lord

- Tell me something Good

- Mirror Him

If this or any of my books has been a blessing to you, please leave a book review on Amazon.com, I would Greatly Appreciate that. To leave a book review, Go to:

amazon.com/author/larryoneal

In addition, you can contact me at: Leonealauthor@aol.com

Made in the USA
Columbia, SC
22 September 2022